To Mary Ann and
The Lourdes Community
For all the educational
value you bring to
our region and to the world

Tom Brady

Plastic Technologies, Inc.
Our Story

By Dr. Tom Brady
Founder and Chairman Emeritus
Plastic Technologies, Inc. (PTI) 1985-2022

This publication contains the ideas and opinions of its author. It is intended to provide helpful and informative material on the topics addressed in the publication and it is based on the author's knowledge and recollection of events, related to the best of his knowledge. Incidents are related to highlight issues and are not intended to portray any given company or individual in a negative light. The author does not assume and hereby disclaims any liability to any party for any loss, damage, or disruption caused by errors or omissions, whether such errors or omissions result from accident, negligence, or any other cause.

Direct any comments or questions or requests for an electronic copy of this book to: drtombrady1944@gmail.com
Bound copies of this book can be purchased from Amazon or from any bookstore

Acknowledgements

A history, by definition, is a collection of memories, analyzed and reduced to meaningful conclusions. This history of PTI, however, is as much a collection of the memories of those who helped me create that history, as it is of my own memories.

John Dunagan deserves a special thanks because it was John who conceived of the Coca-Cola Cooperative coalition in 1985 and it was John who approached me to ask whether I would leave my secure job at Owens-Illinois, Inc. and help the regional Coca-Cola Cooperatives to build a self-manufacture capability. So, I owe John Dunagan a huge thank you for convincing me to leave O-I and to embark on what has been an unbelievably exciting and rewarding 36-year career as the PTI Founder.

I also want to recognize and thank Mr. Tom Ethington who for most of PTI's history was our official company photographer, since many of the photos in this book came from Tom's archives.

Of course I owe this entire history as well as this summary of that history to my wife and best friend, Betsy Brady, who not only enthusiastically encouraged and supported me in this endeavor for the past 36 years, but who also created and managed the administrative, financial, personnel, and cultural aspects of all the PTI companies from the very beginning ….. and, as an English major in college, she served as my very capable editor for this book!

And as will be clear through the course of this book, so many others have been integral to this amazing journey – company leaders, employees, customers, vendors, innovators, supporters, advisors, and partners of all stripes – all their contributions and heartbeats live on through the memories and stories and pictures here – and the PTI of the future which is still being shaped. My deepest appreciation to all who have been a part of My Journey!

Table of Contents

Introduction

After graduating from the University of Michigan in 1972 with a PhD in Materials Engineering, I was hired as a Senior Plastics Technology Associate by **Owens-Illinois (O-I).** I vividly recall my first day at the O-I Technical Center which, as it happened, was a premonition of (what became) the future.

O-I North Technical Center, 1972

My boss, Dr. Jerry Miller, started me out with a tour of the entire O-I Technical Center which, at the time, was where O-I carried out all the R&D for glass, metal, paper, and plastics packaging.

Today, O-I has retrenched to become a glass container business only. Back then, however, O-I was a full-service packaging company with a Plastic Products Division that was one of the leading plastic container producers in the country, with 18 plants nationwide that made polyethylene (PE), polyvinyl chloride (PVC), and polystyrene (PS) containers, closures, and multipack carriers.

As we toured the O-I Glass Container Research Labs I still remember looking through the window into one of the labs where a man standing on a 12-foot ladder and wearing what looked like a protective white space suit was dropping 64 oz glass bottles filled with carbonated liquids to test their resistance to shattering when dropped.

Drop Test - 32 oz (coated) Glass Bottle

I also noted that every bottle shattered and that the man on the ladder always looked away and covered his face with his hands.

I later learned that the protective suit was indeed to shield the technician from exploding glass shards and that the bottles were coated with **Surlyn™** plastic (the same plastic used to coat golf balls!)

Soon after my tour and almost before I was even assigned a desk, I learned from Dr. Miller that Coca-Cola had recently asked O-I and its other packaging suppliers to offer options for "family-sized" containers, so they could sell more product.

12 oz Glass Bottles - 1972

You may recall that the only glass and metal container options back then were 12 oz or smaller because, as it turns out, it is nearly impossible to make large sized metal and glass containers that are both safe and economical.

So, my tour of the O-I Technical Center that first day was indeed a premonition of my 50-year career in the plastic packaging industry. It was obvious already to Dr. Miller and to the other plastics executives at O-I, and even to me after that first tour, that the only way to make family-sized carbonated soft drink containers was going to be to figure out a solution with plastics!

Of course, plastics had never been used for carbonated soft drinks up until that time, because the then-common commodity plastics such as polyethylene (PE), polyvinyl chloride (PVC), and polystyrene (PS) were very permeable to O_2 and CO_2, so they could not offer sufficient shelf life for commodity soft drink packaging. Nor could commodity plastics offer enough strength to resist expansion when exposed to the internal pressures of 60-100 psi found in carbonated soft drinks.

2L PET Bottle with a PE Base Cup

Some of the engineering plastics, like nylon and polycarbonate (PC), did offer somewhat better permeability resistance (nylon) or strength and drop impact resistance (PC) but, they also had their limitations, including having property limitations such as opacity (nylon), or strength and cost (PC). Other package suppliers and material suppliers were, of course, getting the same message from Coca-Cola and from Pepsi-Cola and from all the carbonated soft drink manufacturers. The race to offer a commercial option began just as I walked into my first job at O-I.

As it turns out, I hit the jackpot and was offered the "opportunity of a lifetime." After all, how many people get the chance to help start an entire and lasting industry? Well, let's say that I and my colleagues at O-I got that chance back in the early 1970's and, I am happy to say, we seized the opportunity and "made it happen," which all led to my opportunity to leave O-I in 1985 to create PTI and to continue that journey.

Industry Situation and Early PTI History

If the reader is interested, the entire history of the PET bottle and the sequence of events that motivated me to found PTI are available in my book titled **"History of the PET Bottle,"** also available at Amazon's BookBaby or in other bookstores.

To continue that story in this book, suffice it to say that because O-I was not planning to pursue the PET bottle business I had no real conflict of interest when I left and no real restrictions beyond not sharing competitive information. I was able to leave O-I and to found Plastic Technologies, Inc. (PTI) in December of 1985 (actually, the first name was Midwest Plastic Research Associates), and I did so initially to help John Dunagan and Dick Roswech and the Coca-Cola Company achieve their goal of self-manufacturing their own plastic containers.

In fact, soon after founding PTI, O-I also approached PTI to ask for help in designing a novel rotary preform compression molding machine, which we did.

One trailer to the O-I Plastic Beverage Operations story, which I can only tell now that most of the former O-I glass executives will no longer read this book, is this. About 3 years after I left O-I and founded PTI, I was asked to give a talk at the Rotary Club in Downtown Toledo, which I did, and I used the opportunity to tell the story about the PET bottle.

As I was packing up my sample PET bottles in my brief case after the talk, I looked out into the audience and noticed the former O-I Chairman, Ed Dodd, who had obviously come to hear my speech.

As the room was clearing, Ed Dodd, who had retired from O-I by that time, walked up to the front of the room and looked up at me (I was on a stage), and just said "You know, Tom, we probably should have done that," and then he walked away.

That was the last time I ever saw Ed Dodd, and even today I hold no ill feelings because I understood exactly why O-I made that decision. Indeed, had O-I decided to pursue PET, I would never have had the opportunity to start PTI and to pursue what has turned out to be an exciting and rewarding career as an entrepreneur.

The Evolution of the PET Bottle Industry

The introduction of plastic was indeed the trigger that precipitated the move to self-manufacture in the soft drink industry because, heretofore, the options were only glass or metal and, as it turns out, the significant investment and centralized locations required for glass and metal container manufacturing operations do not lend themselves to distributed self-manufacture.

Plastic package manufacturing machinery, on the other hand, can be easily installed on site right next to the filling operations, which offers total flexibility for manufacturing various sizes and types of containers.

Today, in fact, self-manufacture of plastic packaging is widespread, even beyond the beverage industry, and glass containers are only used today for more specialized packaging applications.

Plastic Can with Roll-on Aluminum Lid

After I left O-I and began working to help Coca-Cola expand their plastic container manufacturing operations and to develop a plastic can that would replace the metal can, I learned that John Dunagan and Coca-Cola had licensed the free-standing petalloid (footed) base technology from Continental PET Technologies and that they were working together with Continental and with Marty Beck in Amherst NH where the Continental R&D Labs were located.

Of course, I did not yet have my own PTI laboratories during those first several years so my job was to work directly with Marty Beck and Continental to help expand the Coca-Cola self-manufacturing operations and to develop a 12 oz plastic can to replace the traditional metal can, so that Coca-Cola could also consider self-manufacturing its own cans, just as they were doing with bottles.

During those first several years after leaving O-I, I got to know Marty Beck and his R&D team well because the Continental labs served as Coke's plastic labs and the

Marty Beck

Continental team, with me as the project manager, served as Coke's technical self-manufacture team.

The CPET team included Wayne Collette, George Rollend, Tom Nahill, Suppayan M. Krishnakumar (Inventor of the petalloid base), Brad Molnar, Richard Clark, and Lou Tacito.

Wayne and Kathleen Collette

George Rollend

Lou Tacito

As the new Coca-Cola self-manufacture technical project manager, I had a chance to look inside the Continental laboratories and to meet the technical team that had been O-I's (my) number one competitor, because now this was my team to make things happen for Coca-Cola, licensor of Continental's PET technology.

To put it mildly, I was very impressed, because the Continental team had developed and patented the one-piece (no base cup required) PET bottle/can base designs and a new multilayer preform injection technology, and Coca-Cola needed both technologies to self-manufacture their own PET bottles and to develop a multilayer, high barrier, plastic 12 oz can.

Pushup base used for the 12 oz can and models of the 1L and 2L Petalloid base designs for bottles

Continental Petalloid (footed) base

Soon after the self-manufacture of beverage bottles happened, Continental, a world leader in the manufacture of metal beverage cans, apparently also began to question the compatibility of owning both plastic container and metal container manufacturing businesses, since those internal businesses competed, as was the case at O-I with glass and plastic.

First PET Plastic Cans

Further, John Dunagan and Coca-Cola began to recognize that the introduction of a plastic PET beverage container in large quantities would stimulate questions about the recyclability of the new plastic PET container. Metal cans and glass bottles were already recognized as being recyclable and, in many parts of the country, recycling was already underway.

However, PET plastic containers represented a new packaging medium for the beverage industry and John Dunagan, Dick Roswech and the Coca-Cola Company recognized early on that they had to address this question or risk a backlash against the introduction of a non-recyclable package at scale.

Perhaps coincidentally, the early consideration by Coca-Cola of how to promote the recyclability of PET and the nearly coincidental considerations by both O-I and Continental to divest of their investments in plastic, led John Dunagan and his Coca-Cola self-manufacture colleagues to hire another project manager to address the question of PET recycling, just as they had hired me to be the project manager for PET container self-manufacture.

Not surprisingly, they decided to approach Marty Beck at Continental to become the PET Recycling Project Manager, just as they had approached me to become the PET Manufacturing Technology Project Manager.

Just as I had made my decision to leave O-I, in part because O-I had become more concerned with the internal competition between plastic and glass, I suspect that Marty, also made his decision to leave Continental because Continental was now becoming more concerned with the internal competition between plastic and metal.

In any case, the fact that both Marty and I happened to leave our respective Fortune 100 plastic packaging companies within a few months of each other and that we found ourselves teamed together to help Coca-Cola self-manufacture their own PET plastic bottles and to develop a viable national recycling strategy, turned into the opportunity of a lifetime for both of us.

Marty and I travelled together, we presented together, we brain-stormed together, we worked together, we gathered together with our families, and we certainly accomplished more together for Coca-Cola and for the PET industry because we joined forces during those early years.

Also, and interestingly, even though we both established independent PET technology development companies and PET manufacturing companies and PET recycling companies (Marty's company was DEVTECH), we never really competed. In fact, we actually contracted overflow work out to each other when we couldn't handle all the work internally, because we respected and trusted each other.

However, most importantly, we had the chance to really get to know one another, to work closely together in an industry that we had jointly helped create, and we were jointly successful at accomplishing the mission(s) that Coca-Cola and John Dunagan had in mind back in 1985.

Marty passed away before his time at age 67 in 2019, but in 2018 as I was assembling my PET bottle history museum in my home shop (perhaps the only such museum in the world!), Marty shared with me several of his prized early PET and acrylonitrile bottle samples which I now have proudly displayed as part of my collection, and as a small tribute to a best friend.

Since Marty's passing, his wife Jane and I have continued to communicate and she also has contributed additional historic plastic bottles to my collection, in memory of Marty. Thank you, Jane!

The Story of Plastic Technologies, Inc. (PTI)

Thomas E Brady, PhD

I founded **PTI** in 1985 because I had an unusual background as the former VP and Director of Plastics Technology for **Owens-Illinois, Inc.** and because, even as a young plastics research engineer, I had been assigned primary responsibility for leading the technical and commercial development of PET bottle technology at O-I during the period 1971-1984.

The premise for creating PTI was that the Coca-Cola bottlers who had embarked on a successful PET bottle self-manufacturing strategy during the period 1981-1984 were seeking to expand their efforts and to undertake the development of new and innovative PET plastic soft drink packaging products, including for example, a PET plastic can. To accomplish these goals, the four Coca-Cola self-manufacturing cooperatives agreed to jointly sponsor and fund several major product development and engineering projects and to hire an experienced individual to manage these projects for the combined cooperatives.

Well known to all the bottlers and managers in the Coca-Cola self-manufacture system because of my previous history and experience in PET technology and in the soft drink industry, I was approached by the Coca-Cola self-manufacture bottling cooperatives about the opportunity to leave O-I and to manage these project development efforts for the Coca-Cola System.

Initially I declined the offer, even though it was an exciting opportunity because, as I recall, I didn't want to just change employers. However, when I decided to make a counter proposal to the Coca-Cola cooperatives to establish a separate independent company for the purpose of managing these projects, the Coca-Cola cooperatives agreed.

I was then able to create a new company, **Midwest Plastic Research Associates Inc. (MPR),** with me as the only employee and I was able to negotiate long-term contract agreements with the four Coca-Cola cooperatives and with the Coca-Cola Company. I signed the incorporation papers on December 23, 1985.

The contracts assured MPR of funding for 4 years and required me to manage the Plastic Can Development project and for MPR to carry out other engineering and technical development projects for the combined Coca-Cola Cooperatives, at their direction.

Midwest Plastic Research Associates' First Office

My first office in Toledo, after I changed the name from Midwest Plastic Research Associates to Plastic Technologies, Inc.

While meeting with my good friend, Jim Kline, at his Shumaker Loop & Kendrick law offices to ask for advice on how to form a new company, we looked out from his 3rd floor office across the street at the offices of Matrix Technologies and Jim said, let me introduce you to Roger Radeloff, the Matrix Technologies Founder and CEO, which he did.

Roger was not only helpful, but he offered me a "free" office in his building located in the Goerlich Building at the corner of Canton & Spielbusch Avenues in Downtown Toledo, just to get started, and as if that were not enough, he also offered me the "free" services of Marilee Spann, his Administrative Assistant.

Marilee and Tim Spann

Both offers turned out to be key to a successful start! The office that Roger provided was in a section of the building where there were 6 other unused offices so I could add employees and Marilee Spann eventually became my full time Administrative Assistant and PTI's (actually, Midwest Plastic Research Associates') first full-time employee.

Following Jim Kline's sage advice, I quickly assembled a Business Advisory Board which, I am pleased to say, was made up of experienced professionals that any Fortune 500 company would like to have on their boards, and they all wanted to help, and all declined to be compensated!

That first board consisted of Jim Kline, Sam Carson (my father-in-law and past CEO and President of the Toledo Trust Company), Frank Harris (another fellow entrepreneur, former O-I employee, and Founder and CEO of AIM Packaging Corporation), Steve Martindale (another independent entrepreneur, CEO of the Kiemle-Hankins Company, and a fellow Dartmouth graduate), and Dr. Les Lahti, (Dean of the University of Toledo College of Engineering).

One of the first pieces of advice I got from that Advisory Board was to "change the name" of the company to something that better reflected the business and a broader industry capability, and to make the change quickly in order to establish an industry brand.

So, within the first 6 months, I studied the options and that was when we became **Plastic Technologies, Inc.** with **PTI** as the logo. Thanks go to my brother-in-law, John Fedderke, a marketing expert who designed the PTI logo that we used for more than 30 years.

My first contracts were with the Coca-Cola Company and the 4 Coca-Cola Cooperatives; Western Container, Southeastern Container, Florida Coke or FlPak, and New York Coke or Apple Container. However, I was quickly contacted by several other companies, and within the first 6 months I signed consulting contracts with The Campbell Soup Company, Great Lakes Canning Corp., Owens-Illinois Inc., Packaging Corporation of America, and Polyseal Corp.

In my first PTI office

As a single consultant with no company labs or technical support, those contracts were more than I could handle but, fortunately, just 6 months after taking off, a former O-I colleague, Bob Deardurff, called me and asked what I was doing. He told me that with O-I's waning interest in PET and plastics, he was bored!

Bob Deardurff

Of course, I was delighted since Bob had been one of my first technical hires at O-I, and with 10 years of experience in exactly what my customers needed, he was a perfect first addition to my team.

I held my breath when I made him an offer that was probably less than he was making at O-I, with fewer benefits, and virtually no job security; but to my great good fortune, he not only said yes but he said that he was ready to start almost overnight! What a relief! I had an office ready to go, so Bob brought his own Macintosh computer (remember those?), and off we went.

After just a few months, we again had more work than both Bob and I could handle, and while Marilee was able to handle the office activity, I quickly learned that running a business required doing all the administrative, financial, legal and personnel things that engineers were never trained to do.

Betsy Brady

Happily, my wife Betsy was very good at organizing and handling all these administrative tasks, and even though she was still taking care of our 3 kids and was involved in many community activities (she was president of the Junior League that year!), she jumped in to help at PTI.

Help probably does not fully describe Betsy's contributions, then or now. In fact, even though she was able to adjust her time at PTI to fit her family schedule early in our history, we have relied on Betsy to lead our administrative, financial, and legal activities from the very beginning.

12

Scott Steele

Not long after, Bob and I found that the engineering workload was growing rapidly, but again by great good fortune, another former colleague of ours at O-I, Scott Steele, called and asked what we were doing! Scott became our third trained and experienced engineer which really helped, but opportunities seemed to triple and word of our little venture seemed to spread rapidly, both in the industry and even to our former employer, O-I.

Fortunately, just as our friends from both Corpoplast and Campbell Soup called to ask for help, and the opportunity to develop our first medical package came in the door, and several joint venture product opportunities emerged, our fourth "founding professional" from O-I, Frank Semersky, showed up, along with two other former and (then) retired O-I colleagues, Albert Uhlig and Jim Berry.

Frank Semersky

Al Uhlig

Bob, Scott, and I enthusiastically welcomed them into our now growing venture and we were off and running!

Al Uhlig was our "Inventor;" Jim Berry was our "Designer." Jim and Al both used a drawing board (remember those?). Frank Semersky was the brains behind our "New Business Development" efforts, and for the next 25 years, Bob, Scott, Frank, and I handled the technical development and consulting projects. Betsy and Marilee "Ran the Office!"

Jim Berry

Betsy Brady and Marilee Spann

13

1987 The Founding PTI Management Team
Albert Uhlig, Betsy Brady, Scott Steele, Tom Brady,
Bob Deardurff, Marilee Spann, Frank Semersky

Our rapidly increasing contractual funding provided the credibility our new enterprise needed to quickly identify additional customers who did not compete with Coca-Cola, and to attract and grow an experienced and ever-broader professional staff to carry out the technical development for the Coca-Cola Cooperatives and for those other early PTI customers.

Interestingly, while I was sitting in my office one day, I was visited by Harley Kripke who was soliciting for the United Way. After agreeing on our annual donation to United Way, we began sharing stories about our respective entrepreneurial businesses.

Harley's father and brothers had owned and operated Omnisource, a very successful scrap metals business in the Toledo area for many years. When Harley learned that PTI was a plastics technology development company, he launched into telling me about an opportunity to recover the copper from electrical wire and cable scrap, but that to do so he would need plastics expertise to deal with the PVC and PE insulation scrap.

As it turned out, that was the start of one of several new PTI joint ventures that fell well outside the plastic packaging industry but, and I will tell the stories later, those excursions outside our primary focus on packaging were important for the evolution of the **PTI Family of Companies**.

Other opportunities that just walked in the door during those first several years included:

- Designing and manufacturing portable plastic entertainment centers
- Designing and licensing a tamper-resistant urine sampling container
- Designing and manufacturing plastic lake dock sections
- Developing the first plastic 3D Printer material for Stratasys
- Designing plastic pipettes for O-I's Kimble Division
- Helping Husky design a commercial blow molding machine
- Acting as the technical expert in 2 major industry lawsuits
- Providing PET technical support to companies in Canada, Japan, and Taiwan

And, we still had 3-year consulting contracts with the Coca-Cola Company and the four Coca-Cola Cooperatives, and Coca-Cola continued to target the manufacture of 100% of its PET bottles; and they still wanted to develop a plastic can!

PTI's First Office/Laboratory Facility

Because we were quickly outgrowing our Goerlich Square office space, and because we also needed to create and fund a laboratory to handle all of the development projects that were coming our way, in 1987 we thanked Roger Radeloff for helping us get started and we moved our growing company into Ken Kloster's Research and Development Center which he had named the "**Menlo Park Innovation Center**," located at 333 14th Street, also in downtown Toledo.

Interestingly, when I was the Plastics Technical Director at O-I, one of my offices had been in that same building which was called "The Duraglas Center," because it had originally housed only O-I Glass R&D employees.

As it happened, when I consolidated the various O-I Plastics R&D Groups from their various locations around Toledo, including from the Duraglas Center to Levis Development Park in Perrysburg OH in 1983-1984, Ken Kloster purchased the Duraglas Center from O-I to house his own vehicle hand tool manufacturing business. Because Kloster Mfg. used only 2 of the 4 floors, Ken Kloster made the 3rd and 4th floors available at very reasonable lease terms, hoping to attract new local startup businesses, hence the name "Menlo Park."

Once we got settled into what we called "The Kloster Building" and once we began putting both PTI Analytical Testing and PTI Processing and Prototyping Laboratories together, our business really accelerated, and we began hiring additional technical personnel to handle the workload, and to address the many apparent business development opportunities that seemed to come our way.

Tracy Momany

Our first University of Toledo engineering student was Tracy Momany who created our first analytical testing laboratory. Tracy also hired our first testing laboratory technician, Keith Brown, who had just left his job as a water quality technician in the Toledo area.

Keith Brown

Tracy and Keith created our first Constant Temperature Room in a mini barn we purchased at Home Depot, and they installed our first laboratory viscometer and Instron mechanical property tester which we inherited from Owens-Illinois.

First Constant Temperature Room

I must, however, digress to tell a very interesting, and to me unforgettable, story about my last day in the Matrix Technologies offices when Roger Radeloff took me to lunch to say goodbye.

As Roger was driving us back to the office, he looked over at me and asked, "Why the heck are you hiring all those people? Employees are just a huge pain in the neck!"

And I also remember very clearly how I answered Roger when I responded, "Roger, I just want to prove that I can make work fun for employees, which is really why I left O-I."

As they say, "the rest is history." We have had 36 years of hard work, much success, a ton of creativity, and lots of fun at PTI, and up until just a few years ago, I liked to say during my public speeches that "I could count on one hand the number of PTI professionals that had left PTI over my 25 years as CEO," which some might say means that we did not hire enough "new blood" over the years, but to me and to our PTI Family of Companies leadership teams, that statistic was a by-product of "hiring good people and then getting out of their way!"

When we moved into the Kloster Building in 1987, we had only 8 employees. When we moved from the Kloster Building to Wolf Creek Executive Park in Holland, OH in 1994, we had 20 employees, many of whom are still with PTI in 2022.

A lot happened between 1986 and 1991, including those early excursions outside the PET packaging industry, but first I want to relate several stories that could have changed the course of history for PTI.

The Red Couch

Only a few who read this will ever remember, or have an appreciation for, the Red Couch!

 Of course, we had little money to spend in those early days on office furniture so my father-in-law, Sam Carson, helped me out by donating some of his old bank office furniture, including what must have been a 50-year-old red leather, and not so comfortable, couch which became the seating in my sparsely furnished office.

While I am not sure a visitor ever even sat on that couch, the Red Couch became the weekly planning spot for Bob, Scott, Frank, and me and we all remember it fondly since when we sat on the Red Couch, we all got serious about planning our next several weeks!

Decision Time

I suppose very few entrepreneurial startups go exactly the way the business plans are written, and I also suppose that most entrepreneurs experience at least one "ah ha" moment as they try to get traction.

Well, my first "ah ha" moment came in 1987 just after we moved into the Kloster Menlo Park Innovation Center when the phone rang and John Dunagan told me that two of the four coops, including both New York Coca-Cola and Florida Coca-Cola, wanted to exit their contracts with PTI.

By that time, Coca-Cola and the Coops had pretty much given up on developing a plastic can and neither Coke New York nor Florida Coke manufactured their own PET bottles, so even though there were still 2 years left on their contracts with PTI, they decided that they wanted to focus their dollars and their attention elsewhere which, in retrospect, was perfectly understandable. They were not critical of PTI and our support. Rather, without the plastic can project, they just did not need the technical services of a company like PTI.

They wanted to just buy out the two years on their contract, which would leave Southeastern Container and Western Container still under 2-year contracts to PTI, and New York and Florida were willing to buy out their contracts for the full 2-year value that they would have paid to PTI. Since the initial 4-year contracts for each of the 4 coops were substantial, it was decision time for me, and for our small management team. If we had just accepted the buyout values of those two contracts, we could have abandoned the business, worked a buyout deal with both SEC and WCC, walked away happy about our two years, and all of us could have secured good jobs elsewhere. However, Bob, Scott, Frank, and I agreed that we were still excited about our new venture so we decided to negotiate a deal with the Coops that would allow us to continue.

To make a long story short, what we finally negotiated with SEC and WCC was that we would apply the buyout money from New York Coke and Florida Coke to future projects for SEC and for WCC, if they would agree to extend our contracts for another two years.

This was a good deal for both SEC and WCC and for PTI because the remaining two coops would get two years of essentially free technical support work from PTI, and PTI would be able to extend our runway to become a sustainable business without depending only upon Coca-Cola for business.

So that is what happened, and I do believe that our decision was a good one for both our founding customers, Southeastern Container and Western Container, and for PTI, since our then-essentially 6-year contracts with SEC and WCC did give us the runway to create a more diverse and sustainable business.

Our second "ah ha" moment happened shortly after we had made that deal and were having a meeting at PTI's new office/laboratory complex in the Kloster Building. We had invited both John Dunagan, WCC President, and Dick Roswech, SEC President, to discuss future plans and strategies and we were meeting in our third-floor offices when a delivery truck showed up with our first injection machine.

We, of course, were terribly proud to show off our developing analytical and process labs to our two biggest customers and we were also delighted that they were with us to watch us unload the injection machine that we had purchased just to help them develop new PET bottles.

But fate intervened! As we all stood by on the loading dock with our two biggest customers to watch the injection machine be moved off the trailer and delivered to our laboratory, disaster struck. The machine suddenly tipped and literally fell off the trailer and crashed down onto the pavement, right in front of our customers, who had helped pay for the machine! You can only imagine how devastated and embarrassed we were!

Here we were, meeting with our biggest customers, bragging about how we were going to help them develop new bottles and lightweight their current bottles, and how this new injection machine was going to be the key to our planned projects, when right before their eyes this important and expensive machine was dumped off the truck and ruined.

That was not a good scenario. We thought we had just demonstrated to our best customers that we didn't even know how to unload a machine, let alone how to install it and how to run it for their projects.

To be perfectly honest, I don't really remember how the rest of the meeting went, or perhaps my mind just refuses to remember. In any case, what I do know is that after the dust all cleared, John Dunagan and Dick Roswech were more than understanding and not only continued to support PTI and our project work for them, but they never really made a big deal about the disaster, and they even extended their contracts for many more years.

PTI continued to "lightweight" their Coca-Cola bottles and as I recall, Coke and the Coops saved $10M for every gram we removed, and in those days, we were eventually able to lightweight Coke's 2-liter bottles from 67 grams to 53 grams, so sticking with PTI turned out to be a good deal for both Coca-Cola and for PTI. However, it still makes me sweat when I think back to that day on the loading dock!

Early Excursions Outside the PET Packaging Industry

To be clear, even though every product and business development opportunity that we explored outside of the PET packaging industry was successful, none of these developments were ever fully commercialized.

At the same time, these development opportunities were both fun and exciting, and they became the entry tickets for many of our early experienced and senior technical personnel.

Also, in retrospect, I will admit that PTI's pursuit of these many diverse opportunities is more a reflection of my own personality and desire to attack almost any opportunity, than it is of a well-planned business strategy (Betsy has always called me a "prospector"). However, in retrospect, I also believe that our pursuit of these opportunities played an important role in our ability to attract the many solid employee/owners that have made PTI successful over our 35-year history. They provided the entrepreneurial environment that led to the many PTI Companies that were commercially successful and which did address important opportunities within the PET packaging industry.

So, let me provide several quick summaries before I talk more about how PTI developed after 1991.

Plastic Recovery Systems (PRS™)

Stacey and Harley Kripke

Our first excursion into recovering the plastic insulation from recycled electrical wire and cable scrap started with the conversation in my office with Harley Kripke. During that conversation we agreed to form Plastic Recovery Systems as a 50:50 joint venture company between Kripke & Associates and PTI for the purpose of developing and commercializing a process to clean, separate, and recover mixed PE and PVC from electrical wire and cable insulation scrap.

The wire and cable scrap which remains after the metal wire has been removed is composed of 70% plastic but is highly contaminated with fiber, copper, aluminum, rubber and other plastics and dirt. In addition, about 25% of the recovered PE scrap is crosslinked, adding to the problem of reclaiming and reusing these plastic resins.

However, since that scrap then went to landfill, it was all available at no cost from just a few wire and cable reclaimers in the country. We believed that there was a huge business opportunity if we could design a process to effectively reclaim that plastic scrap for reuse in secondary products.

Duane Nugent

As it happened, another talented chemical engineer, Duane Nugent, was also just retiring from O-I so we asked Duane whether he wanted to work with us under contract to develop a recycling process.

Happily, Duane jumped at the opportunity and because we had just moved into our new process laboratory, we were off and running.

In just a matter of 6 months, Duane had developed a unique and proprietary process which reclaimed the PE, PVC, and residual metals at purities greater than 99%. The system was unique in that it required only aqueous nontoxic solutions as slurry carriers and because it employed multiphase flow principles, rather than the standard specific density differences, to separate the components.

First prototype plastic wire & cable insulation recovery system

Duane assembled a working prototype/pilot system in our laboratory, and we began producing test quantities of **Poly E™** and **Vinyl T™** resins for evaluation and testing by various potential users.

Mike Zielinski

At about that same time we hired Mike Zielinski, another former O-I engineering colleague, to help us with our Coca-Cola plant support activities. However, with the emergence of the PRS project, Mike also jumped in to help with the prototype molding and Mike eventually assumed responsibility for starting up our first commercial operation in one of the Kripke buildings.

We didn't have molds and machines to make large parts so we used outside molders to prototype various potential products including pallets, steel coil protectors, floor protectors, and road cones, and we even had Goodyear demonstrate that they could reuse the vinyl as new/recycled wire insulation.

Fortunately, we had our own "super model" (Betsy) to demonstrate our new products!

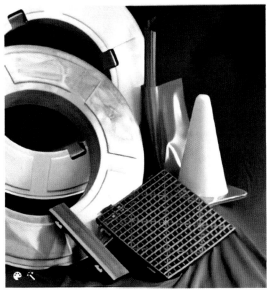
Products molded from 100% wire and cable scrap

*Betsy Brady with some of our first
wire and cable scrap products*

Mike Zielinksi, Duane Nugent, Tom Brady

PT Health Care Products (PTHCP™)

Early in 1987 we were approached by Mr. Ron Newby, one of three principals in PTM, a Professional Telemarketing company located in Lambertville, Michigan that specialized in representing and selling medical testing equipment.

As experienced representatives in the health care market, they were in an excellent position to assess the need for new medical testing products and they had concluded there was a market need for a coded, disposable, tamper-resistant urine sampling container for use in routine drug testing, which had grown dramatically in the past few years.

They had jointly decided to design, produce, and sell such a product but required plastic design and manufacturing expertise.

After discussing the product potential, we agreed to form a joint venture with PTM to design, manufacture, and sell a tamper-resistant urine sampling container, and other such products as the need arose.

We jointly applied for and received a trademark for the name Tru-Container™ and PTI agreed to underwrite the design and patent expenses while PTM underwrote the product marketing, sales, and distribution expenses. We agreed to split any future profits 25% to PTI and 75% to PTM.

Frank Semersky led our development team which included our "inventor," Al Uhlig, who did come up with a unique product design and we applied for a patent on the tamper-resistant feature.

Albert Uhlig, Bob Deardurff, Frank Semersky, Scott Steele, Tom Brady

PTI set about prototyping sample containers. PTM created a sales brochure and approached nine hospitals to seek agreements for supporting an early market test of the product.

Tru Container™

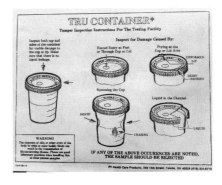

*Patented Tru Container™
Tamper-Resistant Lid*

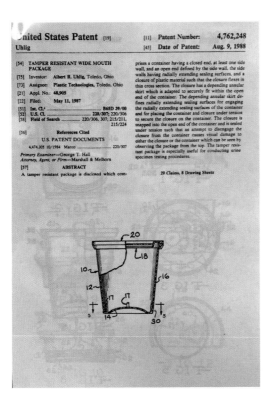

We agreed to share the prototyping and shipping costs as well as the working capital for the project equally, and we agreed that PTI would retain ownership of any intellectual property (IP) but would make it available royalty-free to the joint venture.

A patent did issue within a year and the partners agreed to approach several medical products companies, eventually licensing the design to Becton-Dickinson. Unfortunately, the product never took off, but the business development experience was another valuable lesson for PTI.

First 3D Printer Material for Stratasys

I must tell the whole story behind this "excursion" outside of PET packaging because it really relates to why I started PTI in the first place.

Back at Dartmouth we were introduced to the concept of being an entrepreneur early. In fact, our first engineering course was "Product and Business Development" where we were divided up into teams and given an unsolved problem. Then, the teams were asked to solve the problem, develop a business plan, and then sell that solution at the end of the semester to the Board of Overseers.

Of course, we knew nothing about developing products or starting a business, but that was exactly the point. Before we were immersed in the learning of science and technology, we were asked to learn how to apply engineering thinking to the real world which, by the way, served us all very well. In fact, when I returned for my 15th reunion, half our graduating class had already started businesses!

In any case, our problem was desalinating brackish water. We studied the options and selected reverse osmosis which had just been invented by a man named Srinavasa Sourirajan who lived in Canada and had built his prototype system in his garage.

Well, Canada wasn't so far from Hanover, NH so we hopped into a car and drove up to visit Sourirajan.

We then returned to Hanover, built our own prototype, and I am happy to say, we all passed the course!

The trailer to that story is that when we graduated 4 years later, two of my freshman teammates, Dean Spatz and Chris Miller, stayed for their master's degrees and built a bigger reverse osmosis prototype. When they graduated, they applied for and received venture capital funding from a man named Ralph Crump and they went on to start Osmonics, which eventually became the largest reverse osmosis equipment company in the world!

By the way, they sold Osmonics to GE several years ago, but when I asked for my share of the proceeds, they declined.

In any case, years after we graduated, Dean Spatz was sitting in a bar in Minneapolis having a beer with Ralph Crump's son, Scott Crump, who had just started his own company, Stratasys, which was embarking on the 3D printing technology boom.

Stratasys, by the way, is also now one of the largest 3D printing equipment suppliers in the world!

In any case, as Scott was explaining to my friend Dean over a beer that he was having trouble finding a suitable material for his first 3D printer, Dean said to him, "Why don't you call Tom Brady in Toledo. He is into plastics."

Well, Scott Crump did call me and I, of course, said "Sure, we can figure that out," even though I had no clue what was required! (Remember, Betsy calls me "The Prospector") But, as has happened to make all our other PTI ventures successful, I went out to hunt for my "smart friends and colleagues" who were looking for an opportunity.

This time it was Dr. Frank Schloss who happened to have called me several days earlier wondering what we were doing since, like Bob, Scott, and Frank, he had left O-I and was not having much fun at his current job. So, to make a long story short, I hired Frank on the spot, specifically to take on the Stratasys 3D printer material project, since Frank was a smart chemist and materials scientist who I knew well.

Fortunately, another former O-I colleague, Andy Dickson, who was still hanging on at O-I had also just called to see if PTI could use any of the old O-I plastics laboratory equipment that was now all stored and unused in a building in Perrysburg, Ohio. Happily, Andy took the initiative to see if PTI could use any of that equipment. Well, Andy's offer was a "no brainer" for us since we had little lab equipment and we needed equipment, new or used, desperately. As it happens, one of the pieces of equipment that was available was a two-roll mill/compounder which was used to mix plastic materials in small quantities while they were in the melt state and, as it also happened, a roll mill is exactly what Frank Schloss needed to create resin formulations for the Stratasys project!

Gary Landis and Frank Schloss with the compounding extruder

So, Frank set up a compounding lab and went to work on finding a formulation that would work for Stratasys, and I am again happy to say that within a matter of several months, Frank hit upon a formulation that worked! Frank was ably assisted by Gary Landis, who was our first process laboratory technician.

Unfortunately, PTI resources were already fully committed and invested in our basic packaging business, and we would have had to produce commercial quantities at scale to be successful, which we were not prepared to do.

Frank Schloss in the Materials Lab

Frank did send some of the first quantities to Scott Crump and at the next National Plastics Exposition in Chicago, Stratasys was showing off their new 3D Printing machine and using Frank's resin formulation! For the next year PTI supplied production quantities of the new resin formulation to Stratasys so, it is fair to say that PTI really did invent, manufacture, and sell some of the first 3D printer plastic wire in the world! Eventually, however, Scott Crump and Stratasys developed other formulations and PTI was not needed as a high-volume supplier. PTI did, however, invent one of the first-ever 3D printer materials and that project was my reason for hiring Frank Schloss who spent the rest of his career at PTI and became an owner, a Vice President, and the Director of our Materials Group.

Portare™ Collapsible Entertainment Center Development

In 1990 we were introduced to another local entrepreneur, Tom Pouch, who was a principle in Highland Designs, a company formed for the purpose of developing and commercializing a collapsible portable entertainment center.

Tom Pouch had conceived of and created drawings for a portable bar and had built a prototype using durable materials, including wood panels and metal connecting hardware.

The prototype functioned as the drawing and design explained. It was easily collapsible, and the parts fit together to effectively create a carrying case.

However, the prototype was far too heavy and cumbersome to be used easily at outings or at tailgate parties and Tom Pouch had discovered that the prototype design would be difficult and expensive to manufacture at scale.

He had therefore decided to find a partner that could help him employ lighter weight and moldable plastics to develop a viable commercial product.

I don't recall exactly how Tom Pouch learned about PTI, but he did live in my Sylvania neighborhood, so it is understandable that someone who knew us both had recommended PTI.

In any case, we were intrigued by the possibilities and even though we had no direct experience in rotomolding, we did have significant plastic processing and design experience and we did have appropriate contacts in the contract molding industry.

We signed an agreement and we set about to convert Tom's design to be made from rotomolded parts.

Tom Pouch and Highland Designs applied for a US patent which eventually issued in 1995.

For the reader, rotational molding or rotomolding is a cost-effective production process to form hollow parts of limitless size. Plastic resins in powder form are loaded into a mold that is heated and rotated slowly, both vertically and horizontally. The simultaneous heating and rotation distributes and fuses the powdered resin to the inner surfaces of the mold, leaving the part itself solid but hollow. The result is a final product that is seamless and has a uniform wall thickness, with more material in the corners to absorb shocks and stresses where they occur most. Lightweight and hollow rotomolded parts provide excellent strength, design flexibility, and low cost.

Once we completed the design, we contracted a local rotomolder to fabricate several complete units. After adjusting the final dimensions slightly, we declared success.

Tom Pouch then secured the rights to use several college logos, including from the University of Michigan and Ohio State University, and we decorated the front panels for several of the bars with those logos.

We all then set off to use the **Portabar™** at both UM and OSU tailgate gatherings to see how well they were accepted.

Not surprisingly, the bars were a real hit and any of us who took one to a tailgate gathering was asked repeatedly "where can I get one?"

So, we declared our brief market test a success and then asked ourselves how to commercialize this new product. Tom Pouch did the homework on the capital cost for investing in commercial molds which told us that we would have to invest significant capital and that we would have to mass produce the bars to be successful.

So, once again, we helped jointly develop a really terrific proprietary product but could not divert either our attention or our investment dollars on products that were diversionary from our core package design business.

Once again, our experience with this diversionary product development was very positive and we again learned a lot that has benefited us in many ways over the years.

In retrospect, we should have investigated the venture capital markets for any of these new product ventures, but quite frankly, we were still very new and inexperienced entrepreneurs and we not only had to stay focused on our core PET technology business, but we also were just not sophisticated enough or knowledgeable enough to know how to raise venture capital or how to fund a project with money we did not have ourselves.

More Menlo Park Innovation Center Memories

Alene and Ollie Brownridge

Scott, Tom, Frank, and Bob

Bonnie and Gary Landis

Keith and Julie Brown

Al and Trudy Uhlig

Tom and Betsy Brady

Duane and Irene Nugent

Frank and Sue Semersky

Amy and Scott Steele

Sue and Bob Deardurff

Frank and Willma Schloss

Todd and Tracy Momany

29

Marilee and Tim Spann

Joan and Dan Durham

Menlo Park Display Case

Menlo Park Tenants Sign

Celebrating PTI's United Way Donation

In 1989 Tom and PTI received the Northwest Ohio Ernst & Young Entrepreneur of the Year Award

The Move to Wolf Creek Executive Park

PTI Facility at Wolf Creek Executive Park 1994-1997

As PTI's technical staff expanded and as the revenue base grew at compound annual rates of 35%, the company moved in 1994 from its rented office facility in downtown Toledo to a larger development facility in the suburb of Holland, Ohio where we upgraded our analytical testing and processing laboratories and expanded our PET container and preform prototyping capabilities.

During this period of rapid growth and expansion PTI broadened its customer base and became involved in the development of several diverse business and product opportunities, including health care products, plastic recycling, specialty compound development, and leisure products. In 1997, we built a much larger custom office and laboratory space across the street which houses the current PTI headquarters and laboratories, and which has been further expanded several times to accommodate the company's continued evolution.

PTI Facility at Wolf Creek Executive Park built in 1997

The excursions outside the PET packaging field provided a basis for PTI to hire additional experienced technical professionals, to staff its laboratories and to establish a reputation in the plastics industry as a substantial technical development company. In addition, diversifying the business provided PTI with the opportunity to learn more about technical product and business development.

32

In the end, however, PTI reconfirmed that its longer-term opportunities were in the PET technology business and today, while we still engage in an array of diverse plastics packaging industry technologies, our expertise and resources have been best focused on establishing PTI as the number one independent PET technology development and technical service resource in the world.

2009 PTI Management Team

Scott Steele, Frank Schloss, Donald Miller, Dan Durham, Tom Carros, Tom Brady, Tracy Momany, Bob Deardurff
Seated: Don Hayward, Betsy Brady, Frank Semersky

From 333 14th Street in downtown Toledo
to 1465 Timberwolf Drive in Wolf Creek Executive Park

Our builder was Bostleman Corp

Don and Scott planning

Bob already organized

Tracy planning her office

Frank talking to a customer

Our new process lab

Marilee settling into her new office

Betsy already working

Scott's new office

Sumit Mukherjee joins PTI

Tom and Betsy admiring our new home

1465 Timberwolf Drive

We outgrew our 1465 Timberwolf Drive facility in just 1-1/2 years
and built another new building at 1440 Timberwolf Drive,
also in Wolf Creek Executive Park.

Breaking ground with Ken Minichiello, Construction Manager, and Dick Bostleman, owner of Bostleman Corporation

Today PTI offers Industry Training and Education

Computer Design and Simulation

 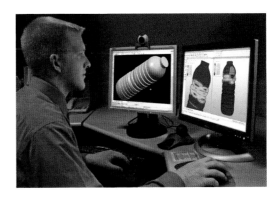

State-of-the-Art Prototyping and Processing

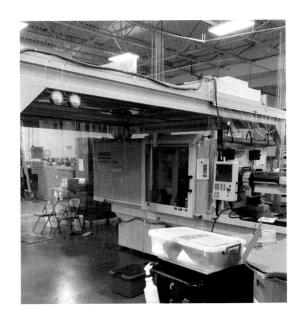

Analytical Material and Product Testing

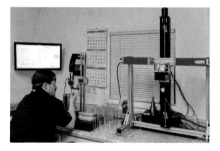

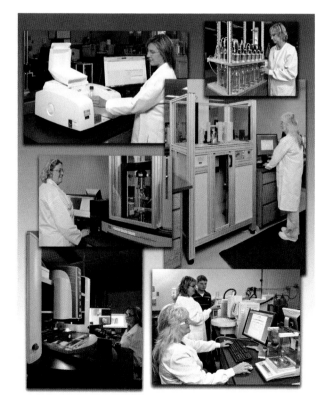

Specialty Instrumentation Development

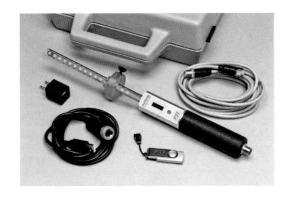

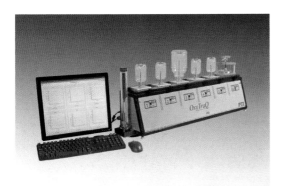

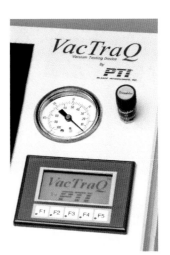

....and PTI has produced more than 150 US and international patents for PTI and for PTI customers.

PTI offers an attractive work environment for PTI employees and for PTI customers who regularly come to work in our labs.

....and PTI employees have developed thousands of packages and containers for customers around the world for the past 36 years!

Handled bottles

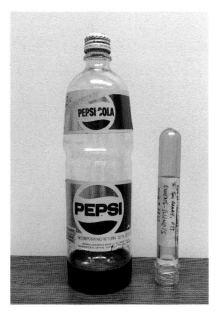

First O-I Bottle and Preform - 1976

Dromo^{TM} Shippable Packaging

Award winning Mountain Dew Package

oPTI™ Foam Technology

Special Promotional Packages

Bottles, Preforms, and Blow Mold

Cold Fill Bottles

Hot Fill Bottles and Preforms

Specialty Packaging

47

Proprietary oPTI™ Foam Technology

Integral Handle Features

Package in a Package

Recycle content containers

Packages Designed by PTI

FiCel ™ Technology

Wine Containers and Glasses

Award Winning Package Designs

oPTI ™ Foaming Technology

From Shampoos to Toothpaste

Household and Personal Care Containers with Recycle Content

Oriented Polypropylene Containers

Tervis™ Insulated Containers made from Tritan™ Copolyester Resin

Single Serve Packaging

Capsule Packaging

3D Printed Containers and Models

50

Ameristar Package of the Year Award

Aerosol Containers

Polypropylene Capsules

Grip Features

PTI Packages

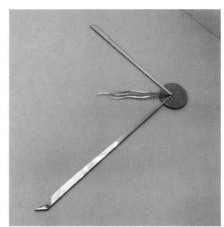

A true, story!

Betsy Brady and Dan Buelow feeding our PTI pigs!

Our contractor did a great job with our new 1440 Timberwolf Drive Wolf Creek Executive Park building, but after we moved into the building, the landscape company did not show up to put in the lawn. The contractor's project manager had moved on to other things, so our gorgeous new headquarters sat in the middle of a mud pit for months and into the next spring.

To get their attention, our maintenance supervisor, Dan Buelow, came back late one night and fenced in a small area right by the front door to our building so that everyone, including our contractor who was headquartered just down the street, could see it. He then borrowed several pigs from a local farmer and placed them in his makeshift pen so that we and the contractor's employees would arrive the next morning to see the pigs happily enjoying their mud pit, which was supposed to have been grass.

Dan's ploy to get the contractor's attention was "a squeal" (pun intended)! The pigs loved their new home, and someone posted a big sign right above their pen that said, "Our new home until the mud is gone!"

Fortunately, this scene did get the project manager's attention and before the newspaper could come out and take pictures, they got busy and pulled out all the stops to get the landscaping done.

Dan took the pigs back home to their farm, but the whole thing was hysterical – and clever – it had us all doubled over with laughter for days although we never found out whether the project manager or the landscaper were as embarrassed as they should have been . . . . but it worked.

Ah, the good old days with creative, entrepreneurial solutions for everything, from everyone! That one always brings back instant laughter.

Growing the PTI Enterprise

While every one of those early "*intra*preneurs" helped me to create PTI and to create the PTI Companies that followed, during the years 1987 to 1995 we brought on board many additional young engineers and administrators who really helped secure the future of our enterprise, and I am happy to say that most of those early young employees remained with and became senior PTI professionals and administrators.

Tom & Betsy 2020

I must also take this opportunity to give special recognition to my wife, Betsy. While I and my PTI colleagues were very good at providing technical development and manufacturing services to our customers, we did not have the time nor the skills to organize and manage the administrative side of the business, including organizing our human resources, handling our financial and administrative services, and becoming what I like to call "the soul of our business," a role which Betsy Brady has filled since the beginning.

Perhaps as importantly, it was Betsy who encouraged me to leave a secure VP job at a Fortune 100 company with 3 young children still at home and with essentially no business experience, to take advantage of what turned out to be a once-in-a-lifetime opportunity. Had she told me that it was too risky and that I had better focus on having a secure job and raising our kids, I would not have made the leap. Thanks, Betsy!

As PTI focused on important development programs for the Coca-Cola Cooperatives and for several other newer customers, PTI and its professional staff quickly established a reputation in the industry as a high-quality PET R&D and technical support resource, and this reputation provided the platform to expand our technical staff, to begin training our next-generation management team, and to create first class analytical testing and processing laboratories.

It is therefore appropriate to recognize those early employees, many of whom earned equity ownership in our enterprise and are still with PTI today.

Qualifying for equity ownership, by the way, was solely my decision in the very early days, but we quickly moved to a system where any Senior Staff member/owner could nominate any other employee, without regard to position or years of service, and then that nomination would be reviewed and either approved or not by the entire Senior Management Team, based solely on whether or not that nominee was viewed as someone who was committed to and had demonstrated the potential to make PTI successful in the future.

Ownership, therefore, has been a subjective decision made by the senior equity owners for most of the history of PTI. This system has served PTI well and over our 36-year history, more than half of all PTI employees became equity owners in PTI.

Tracy Momany

Two of our earliest young engineers who have played key roles at both PTI and the PTI Companies over the years are Tracy Momany and Dan Durham. Tracy joined PTI as one of the first University of Toledo engineering student interns (there was not an official coop program yet) and after interning at PTI while we were still located in the Kloster Menlo Park Innovation Center, she joined full time after graduating with a BS in Chemical Engineering. Tracy has been a key product development specialist for her entire career, and she served as Vice President of Product Development for many years. In 2018, Tracy accepted the position of Manager of Operations of our newest PTI joint venture company and is now the CEO of Guardian Medical USA, Inc.

Dan Durham also graduated from the University of Toledo, but with a degree in Physics. He began his career at another local technical startup company, Tri-Tech, until joining PTI in 1993. Dan has been a key project and customer management engineer over his career and helped found and start up our Preform Technologies LLC company. Today, he remains a key senior marketing and business development professional at PTI.

Dan Durham

Tracy Momany and Dan Durham

Both Dan and Tracy became substantial equity owners. Both were responsible for developing the next $1M PTI customers as we diversified from PTI's early dependence on Coca-Cola, and both have been important contributors to the creation and successes of our PTI Family of Companies. Other employees who joined PTI in the 1987-1993 timeframe when we were still located in the Kloster Menlo Park Innovation Center include Keith and Julie Brown, Lori Yoder, Oliver Brownridge, Diane Ley, and Gary Landis. Keith became our Analytical Laboratory Manager, Lori Yoder was a successful Senior Project Manager and supervised our Materials Development Laboratory, and Diane Ley efficiently handled, and still handles, all PTI's accounts payables and receivables.

Lori Yoder

Ron and Diane Ley

PTI's Materials Development Laboratory

This story and review are courtesy of Dr. Frank Schloss, PTI Vice President and Manager of Materials Development

PTI's Materials Development Department initially led by Dr. Frank Schloss and Ms. Lori Yoder, and now by Dr. Wei Zhang, deserves special recognition as I tell the story of PTI, because even though PTI made its name initially doing innovative package development, the industry has also counted on PTI to innovate when it comes to selecting and creating materials to use in those innovative packages, going all the way back to the development of the first StrataSys 3D printer material.

As the growth spurt of PET accelerated into the 1990s, PTI played a significant role in assisting the leading PET resin manufacturers to evaluate and expand their resin portfolios. During the 1990's, for example, significant development took place to expand and increase the properties of PET so that this highly successful and available packaging plastic could be used for even more rigorous oxygen and heat sensitive packaging applications including for beer and for hot fill applications.

During these exciting development times, PTI carried out confidential and proprietary development work for all the major PET resin companies including Goodyear, Celanese, Eastman, Shell, DAK, Indorama, and M&G. PTI also helped these resin companies to qualify many new PET copolymer compositions that were created using napthalates and PTA (purified terephthalic acid), which could enhance the properties of conventional PET materials.

Another unique comonomer explored by several of these companies was isosorbide, a comonomer derived directly from corn. Isosorbide, as it happens, was one of the earliest PET comonomers that could be naturally derived from plants, and its incorporation as a comonomer with PET eventually resulted in significant improvements to the heat resistance of PET.

During this same time, another bio-derived polyester known as PLA (polylactic acid) was developed and was investigated as another bio-based plastic that could be used for rigid packaging.

PLA is derived from the fermentation of corn sugar, which produces lactic acid, and which then can be polymerized to form long chain plastic PLA molecules.

Cargill invented PLA, then joined with Dow Chemical, an experienced plastic manufacturer, to commercialize this new plastic material and to explore whether it could become a sustainable and bio-compostable polymer suitable to compete in some PET applications. PLA found some early success in the fiber and film industries. When Cargill-Dow decided to explore PLA's application to rigid/bottle packaging, they came to PTI.

Because of PTI's reputation in the industry and even though we had never before worked with bio-derived materials, Cargill and Dow approached PTI to ask if we would assist them in evaluating their formulations and to determine how changing the D/L-ratio of lactic acid would impact the processibility of PLA, with the goal of developing a PLA that could be injection molded into preforms and then reheat-blow molded to form bottles.

This first bio-based plastic materials project was a big challenge for PTI from the beginning because we recognized that we could not expect a PET preform design to also work for PLA. Rather, we first had to determine the processibility and strain-hardening characteristics of these new PLA materials so that we could predict optimum preform designs, as we had done for PET.

However, Lori Yoder jumped into the project and led the PTI and Cargill-Dow development team to progress from initially producing an inconsistent and rather ugly yellow bottle, to consistently producing very nice-looking bottles through the reheat-stretch-blow molding process.

PTI's contributions paved the way for Cargill-Dow to develop a commercial grade PLA in under one year, which they continue to sell into niche water bottle markets, including for use in the very successful BIOTA bottle.

Although the development of a commercial grade of PLA was a technical development success, the ultimate commercial success of PLA in the container market was limited by PLA's substandard water retention properties and PLA, therefore, never made a significant impact on the emerging PET water bottle market.

However, PLA today is successfully being used for many flexible packaging applications and it is fair to say that PTI made a significant contribution to the commercial success of the first corn-based plastic, PLA!

With the success of the PLA development as a barometer, PTI has continued to play a role in evaluating biopolymers for the packaging industry over many years, and other biopolymers or bio-derived traditional polymers, including polyhydroxyalkanoate (PHA), polyhydroxybutyrate (PHB), biobased polyethylene and furan (PEF) based materials were also evaluated by the materials group at PTI. These programs focused on determining optimal processing methods for both melt processing and bottle fabrication, in addition to understanding the optimum preform and bottle designs.

The PTI development team's goal has always been to take full advantage of each new material's properties and to develop packages that could also be made commercially on (then) state-of-the-art manufacturing equipment. Bio-derived monoethylene glycol, for example, became a viable replacement for 30% of the PET molecule when the Coca-Cola Company commercialized their trademarked PlantBottle™.

To this day, PTI's materials development focus continues to be on developing sustainable raw materials and sustainable plastic solutions, and because of the early leadership of Dr. Frank Schloss and Lori Yoder, and the continuing leadership of Dr. Wei Zhang, PTI remains well-positioned to play a key role in today's evolving packaging industry.

PTI Recycling Development Activities

This story and review are courtesy of Dr. Frank Schloss, PTI Vice President and Manager of Materials Development

Recycle Content Containers

As the PET bottle market rapidly expanded during the early 1990's, organizations such as the US-based APR (originally known as The Association of Postconsumer Plastic Recyclers and now known as The Association of Plastic Recyclers), NAPCOR (National Association for PET Container Resources) and PETCORE (PET Container Recycling Europe) were all actively engaged in promoting the recyclability of PET bottles. These organizations initially focused on finding ways to remove PVC (polyvinyl chloride) bottles from the PET recycle stream because PVC caused the PET to degrade and to discolor, affecting the quality of the recycled PET.

Also, in the early days of the industry, the PET resin and additive manufacturers were rapidly developing new and improved grades of PET, and they were developing multilayer barrier materials as well as performance-improving additives, all of which were intended to expand the performance attributes of PET bottles. The problematic issues caused by PVC coupled with these other resin and additive developments raised major concerns among the PET reclaimers that the viability of recycling PET could be in jeopardy.

From the very beginning PTI was actively engaged with these industry organizations to better understand the challenges of recycling PET bottles. PTI's Dr. Frank Schloss worked with NAPCOR to investigate the use of UV (ultraviolet) light to visually detect PVC bottles and ground PVC flake since PVC fluoresces when exposed to UV light. He also was instrumental in the development of improved PVC contamination test methods that were based on PVC's thermal instability which caused visible charring at normal PET processing temperatures.

PTI's Dr. Anne Roulin, Managing Director of PTI-Europe, also worked simultaneously with PETCORE to develop the industry's first standard PET recycle test protocol.

PTI's involvement in the development of these early recycled PET test methods positioned PTI to take a leading role in helping the entire PET industry to better understand the issues affecting PET recyclability.

We also learned early on that performing recycle studies at reclaimer plants was not a feasible option since extremely large quantities of trial materials were required and because such studies resulted in production line disruptions. These issues created a need for small-scale recycling equipment that could replicate production recycling lines, but which only required 50 to 100 lbs. of trial materials for the necessary studies.

While PTI already had developed excellent small-scale resin evaluation capabilities using our Arburg injection presses and Sidel blow molding machines, PTI needed additional capabilities to fully take on project activities that simulated the recycling processes in commercial use.

Kice Elutriator

PTI's Dennis Balduff was instrumental in acquiring the necessary equipment, including a grinder capable of reducing bottles to flakes, a Kice air elutriation device to remove fines from the ground bottle flake, a small-scale solid-stating rotary vacuum dryer, and most importantly, Dennis developed a versatile wash tank capable of simulating the hot caustic wash and rinse used in the industry.

One of PTI's Arburg injection presses was converted into a single screw extruder that, when coupled with a die, water trough, and pelletizer, completed the list of machinery needed to simulate a small-scale commercial recycling line. PTI was then able to offer the industry a laboratory fully capable of performing small scale recycle experiments on PET resins, additives, coatings, multilayer bottles, and labels.

Abbe Rotary Vacuum Dryer

Custom Wash Tank

Realizing that the resin companies had only limited quantities of a new material available for recycle evaluation, PTI's Jason Haslow developed a one-of-a-kind small continuous nitrogen flow, screw-agitated device capable of solid-stating as little as 500g of pellets. When coupled with PTI's developing small scale lab wash capabilities that required only 500-2000g flake quantities, Jason's small solid-stater allowed PTI to become the industry's one-stop shop for running small scale recycle studies whenever only limited amounts of material were available.

PTI was also instrumental in working with the APR, Eastman Chemical, and Wellman to create the first U.S. test protocol for recycled PET, by employing the original PETCORE protocol developed previously by Dr. Roulin. At the time, the APR had qualified only one HDPE test method and only a few laboratory tests to evaluate specific properties of interest to PET.

Today, however, the increased need by brand owners to make their packaging sustainable and recyclable has dramatically increased the need for additional testing which has resulted in the APR developing a much-expanded list of test protocols that can now examine PET thermoforms, polypropylene rigid packages, polyethylene tubes and films, labels, adhesives, and inks. Additional tests have also now been developed to determine a package's recyclability based on the package size, whether it can be detected by NIR (near-infrared spectroscopy), and the presence of ferrous and non-ferrous metals in or on the package.

PTI's recycling team continues to provide consulting and testing expertise and to engage with the "APR Working Groups" responsible for identifying recyclability parameters. PTI also continues to help develop tests and procedures and to be an important support resource for the packaging industry's strategic goal of achieving packaging sustainability through recyclability.

PTI Design, Tooling, and Simulation Services

This story and summary are courtesy of Mr. Sumit Mukherjee, PTI Chief Technical Officer who in a prior role was Director of PTI's Computer Aided Design and Simulation Services and currently also serves as Vice President of Engineering Services

PTI was founded with the goal of providing a wide range of services to the packaging industry and it was with this objective in mind that we embarked on an initiative to add computer-aided design and simulation services to the portfolio of PTI offerings.

Rob Groll

In the very early days, PTI designed preforms and bottles for Coca-Cola by creating large D & E size blueprints using T-square drafting tools. However, working with increasingly sophisticated clients required that PTI modernize its drafting methods and technologies which is what first stimulated us to acquire AutoCAD software more than 20 years ago. Rob Groll, Manager of PTI's Design Group, spear headed those initial efforts and AutoCAD was so successful that Rob soon recommended that PTI acquire even more state-of-the-art SDRC Ideas Software which evolved further under the current ownership of Siemens and is branded as NX Design Software.

With the introduction of plastic carbonated soft drink bottles into the commercial marketplace, the dimensional stability of pressurized plastic containers became a priority and that required an even deeper understanding of the key geometric features of pressurized containers. As some of you may recall, pressurized plastic container designs initially utilized a separate polyethylene base cup which was glued onto the spherical or hemispherical bottom of the highly oriented PET bottle. These early base cup bottle designs required the development of a much more detailed understanding not only of the bottle finish (threaded opening) features, but also of the base cup attachment/locking features. And the dimensional tolerances required to maintain volume, perpendicularity, and shelf-life performance specifications represented significantly greater challenges to the creation of design prints that would define functional pressurized containers over a wide range of shelf-life conditions.

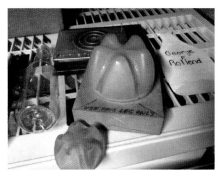
Pushup base used for the 12 oz can and the Petaloid base design used for bottles

Eventually, as more functional pressure-resistant bottom designs were developed, the brand owners began demanding one-piece containers without a base cup. As a result, the plastic bottle suppliers raced to develop functional and proprietary base designs which would resist internal pressure when filled with carbonated beverages, but which would also guarantee empty bottle stability during high-speed manufacture and line-handling.

60

Continental's footed "petaloid" base design emerged as the first successful one-piece bottle design for large diameter containers which, of course, stimulated every bottle maker to develop its own version of the petaloid bottom, while trying not to infringe on the Continental 5-foot base patent.

Bottle designers and manufacturers quickly learned, however, that all one-piece petaloid bottle/bottom designs did not perform the same, either on the lines during the manufacturing process or in the field after filling. With the extensive use of line lubricants to facilitate friction free movement of large quantities of bottles on a high-speed conveyor line, the industry quickly found out that residual surfactants on the unoriented and partially oriented bottle base sections initiated "stress cracking," causing breakage and leakage during transportation, or while in warehouses, and even on store shelves.

This unanticipated condition led to huge research efforts by all manufacturers to invent base designs and to find line lubricant compositions and that would not cause stress cracking.

It was about this same time that PTI was investing in advanced simulation tools which, fortunately, provided the platform for developing a more scientific understanding of petaloid base designs and the resulting bottle and base deformation under high pressures and temperatures.

Also fortunately, PTI had already made great strides in the development of computer simulation and performance algorithms for plastic containers by having recruited Dr. Long Fei Chang from the University of Toledo Polymer Institute. Dr. Chang in his early days at Owens Illinois had worked with Dr. Tom Brady to come up with unique models of polymer processing and container performance and because O-I had abandoned the PET plastic bottle business, PTI was able to utilize Dr. Chang's knowledge and expertise without any conflict of interest.

With the development of even faster and more sophisticated blow molding and injection molding machines came even more complex bottle and preform design challenges which could only be correlated and understood using computer simulations. There was, for example, an emerging need to understand the effects of shear heating and polymer rheology on residual stresses in PET preforms, and PTI emerged as a leader in developing unique computer models for understanding the generation, distribution, and the impact of AA (acetaldehyde) on product taste and bottle performance.

Melted polymer residence time and pressure drop in optimized multicavity injection hot runner manifolds could now be predicted for multi-cavity injection molds where all the preform cavities would be guaranteed to fill simultaneously and to generate the same residual stress distribution in as many as 192 cooled preforms in one injection mold, an accomplishment that no manufacturer had been able to achieve previously. This capability was PTI's key to meeting some of the requirements of the beverage companies whose products were sensitive to taste. Because the shelf life of the package was itself dependent on the IV (molecular weight) preservation, it was important to guarantee reproducible and manageable dimensional growth and burst performance of the resulting bottles.

When it came to optimizing and increasing the speed of the orientation blow molding process, the incorporation of quartz heating lamps in the near IR range of energy emission radically changed the heating efficiency of preforms. Using computer design and simulation technology, PTI developed algorithms which could predict the absorption of energy through the thickness and along the length of the preform. The preform temperature profile could then be controlled by automatically adjusting the wattage of the lamps and the type of filaments used in the blow molding machine.

These leading edge PTI computer simulation models converted the relatively "black art" of preform heating into a more precise science which used Planck's Law for radiation in conjunction with the physics of reflecting surfaces that amplified the heating source and improved the overall blow molding speed and efficiency. The industry soon realized that not only the infrared emission spectra of the IR lamps, but also the absorption characteristics of the PET resin, were important to achieving a uniform preform temperature distribution prior to blow molding. PTI's sophisticated understanding of the heating characteristics of PET eventually led the PET resin companies to develop various grades of PET resin that improved heating efficiency without affecting clarity.

Sumit Mukherjee

All this work was the precursor to the development of PTI's Virtual Prototyping Software modules and to the hiring of Mr. Sumit Mukherjee who led the development of an even deeper understanding of container performance using Finite Element Analysis (FEA) techniques.

The use of FEA involved designing a preform on a computer screen using iterative algorithmic design/performance simulation to achieve the optimum material distribution efficiency after properly reheating the preform. The interaction of FEA with the 3D CAD models allowed us to map the material orientation and thickness of any resulting container in a matter of minutes, without ever making and testing a prototype.

The next step involved applying different loading (internal pressure, or top load, or drop impact) conditions by computer to a computer model of the container to simulate real-world application scenarios and to then simulate and predict the performance of that container under (essentially) real-world conditions. Being able to design and manufacture and test a particular preform/bottle design using a specific PET resin gave PTI a huge advantage in the very competitive PET package development arena.

Aaron Bollinger, Sumit Mukherjee, and Daniel Applegate

Thanks to PTI's design and simulation team, PTI was able to virtually and reliably arrive at a preform and container design using CAD and FEA faster than and with fewer iterations than any of PTI's competitors and before the commercial launch of that container.

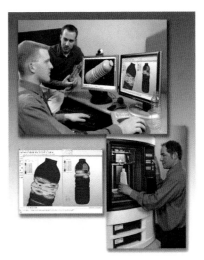

Since PTI's corporate goal was to provide 360-degree coverage for its customers' package development efforts, the tooling department also played a huge role in converting these preform and bottle designs into metal molds that could be rapidly manufactured to produce actual sample preforms and bottles for testing, and in a matter of hours, not weeks. The initial concept of rapid unit cavity injection tooling was envisioned by one of PTI's founding engineers, Robert Deardurff.

Gary Weaver

Gary Weaver, Manager of PTI's Tooling Services, oversaw the efforts to use the CNC (Computerized Numerical Controlled) lathes and 4/5 axis milling machines to quickly fabricate not only injection and blow mold tools but also to create custom fixtures and brackets that would improve efficiency.

Initially we employed epoxy molds to improve speed but newer technologies involving 3D printed molds have now been employed at PTI to rapidly make samples, and PTI now has in-house 3D printing capabilities with the ability to print a wide array of parts, including container mockups and functional parts like grippers and gauges. PTI's Tooling Services Department also provided huge value to the innovation process where new devices and fixtures could be designed and manufactured in much shorter development times, so that trying new ideas and concepts has become almost routine at PTI.

It is also worth emphasizing that short turn-around times for making slight modifications and adjustments to tooling "on the fly" has been a huge asset to PTI's customers who routinely work side-by-side with PTI engineers, designers, and tooling services personnel in PTI's laboratories to create and try out new designs.

With all these current and future enhancements and our continued focus on automation and accuracy, the mission of the PTI Design, Simulation, and Tooling Team is to quickly produce parts that can help a customer's decision-making process and to help that customer carry out a flawless product launch.

PTI Manufacturing Support

This summary was provided by Mr. Donald Miller, PTI Vice President and Manager of Manufacturing Support & Training

Donald Miller measuring preform temperatures using IR

PTI's plant support team is available to provide a range of services to assist in plant startup and/or production, including Final Acceptance Testing (FAT) for new machinery, process optimization, facility audits, product quality control, on-site training, energy savings, and more. And PTI can provide support in person as well as virtually.

In addition to product design and development, PTI has offered manufacturing support services to its customers from the founding of PTI, when PTI provided the Coca-Cola self-manufacturing system with planning, design, and production support as they began the self-manufacture of their plastic beverage containers. Today PTI provides manufacturing support services routinely to all PTI customers who need the support.

PTI was founded by employees who already had extensive plant experience which allowed them to support the needs of PTI's customer base, but today PTI employees not only provide manufacturing support, they also train PTI customers to operate and maintain their own manufacturing operations.

Bob Deardurff's (PTI's first employee) first assignment was to organize a controlled approach to process improvement of injection molded preforms at Western Container, and Scott Steele (PTI's second employee) immediately followed Bob to provide blow molding support at Western Container, by reviewing the equipment and providing direction on how to improve the reheating of the preforms. I was the Technical Manufacturing Specialist at Western Container back then, so I know how helpful that support was!

Frank Semersky (PTI's third employee), who by the way welcomed the challenge to calculate numbers faster in his head than anyone who used a calculator, first introduced the Coca-Cola self-manufacturing system to the routine application of statistics to control manufacturing processes. Frank's early application of statistics to the control of manufacturing processes that previously had depended upon trial-and-error control methods, led PTI to introduce the early and routine application of Statistical Process Control (SPC) and Design of Experiments (DOE) to all the Coca-Cola self-manufacturing operations, and eventually to all PTI manufacturing customers. Frank was also instrumental in introducing SPC and DOE to the American Glass Research Company when they first developed instrumentation to measure the quality of plastic preforms and bottles at high speeds online. In fact, the implementation of online statistical process control, which I attribute directly to Frank Semersky's influence, was so effective that the American Glass Research Company eventually changed their official name to AGR to move away from their historical connection with the glass industry and so they could better serve the plastics industry.

When stress cracking was first identified as a potential problem for oriented PET bottles and particularly for the one-piece "footed" petaloid bottles which were not so highly oriented, PTI was at the forefront of addressing this concern and in developing a manufacturing support service that included reviewing the manufacturing sites, analyzing crack formation, and developing and recommending quality control test methods that are still used in the industry today. This new and necessary quality control support service led PTI to provide support not only to customers in North America but also to customers around the world, as PET packaging became the material of choice for carbonated beverages.

Interestingly, PTI's early development of statistical process control and testing procedures also led to the need for AGR to develop a laboratory device to measure the performance of PET packaging under pressure which eventually led AGR to develop a laboratory burst tester to measure expansion and burst performance of plastic bottles, which has now become standard in the industry.

PTI continues today to provide ongoing plant support to customers by either supporting projects that start at PTI and then following them into production or by responding to requests for support from customers who may not have developed packages at PTI but who must address manufacturing problems or must learn how to reduce costs by optimizing processes.

PTI laboratory and manufacturing support personnel work closely with customers' plants to provide support from an engineering and package development perspective and to assist with processing operations while recognizing the quality control parameters.

Today, PTI has developed the reputation of being an experienced but independent resource that will review manufacturing problems objectively and will provide direction and recommendations for every aspect of a PET bottle manufacturing operation, from resin and additive selection and handling, to drying, injection molding, and blow molding processing, to specifying and operating a quality control laboratory. Other related PTI manufacturing support services available at PTI's laboratories in Holland, Ohio include resin analysis, preform and package performance testing, blow mold sampling, prototyping, and tooling procurement and maintenance.

Over the past 36 years, PTI has expanded its manufacturing support services to customers to include; preparing manufacturing proformas, establishing product specifications, designing and planning complete production lines, providing facilities and building maintenance support, developing detailed systems engineering recommendations, evaluating, specifying, and installing manufacturing equipment, recommending and helping to implement production records and documentation, developing and installing complete quality control laboratories and systems, providing startup and commissioning assistance, providing manufacturing operations training, and conducting energy audits that result in process improvements and air consumption reduction.

Most of PTI's manufacturing process support falls somewhere between "firefighting" and "long-term preplanned support" and may include everything from project management of a new installation to the successful transfer of experimental processes into existing plant operations. In fact, because a manufacturing support project can require anything from one day to several months, PTI's manufacturing support team is focused on transferring knowledge to the customer and on teaching customers the "science" of manufacturing so that they will be better able to handle emergency manufacturing issues.

PTI is one of only a few service providers with the diverse knowledge and experience to deal with almost every aspect of a manufacturing operation since most equipment service technicians are trained only to work on the equipment that their company produces, and PTI's manufacturing support team is proud of the philosophy that has made them successful over the last 36 years and which can best be shared as their team's "mottos":

"Listen to the customer, even if the customer is not able to explain his real need"

"Exceed Every (customer's) Expectation (E^3)"

"Treat every customer's problem as if it is our own problem"

At the end of the day, PTI's manufacturing support team has proven that abiding by these mottos leads to long-term relationships and to becoming a "trusted advisor" for customers.

PTI Industrial Training Courses

This summary was provided by Mr. Donald Miller, PTI Vice President and Manager of Manufacturing Support and Training

Donald Miller Training at PTI

Because PET bottles were still relatively new to the plastics industry and because the technologies for manufacturing PET preforms and bottles were very different from the technologies for manufacturing polyethylene and PVC bottles, PTI was able to fill an industry niche early on by developing an industrial PET technology training program and by employing the same standard teaching methods that were commonly used in our K12 schools; that is we used overhead projector slides, prepared written handouts, asked PTI professionals to deliver lectures, and asked our customers to spend several days in a PTI classroom.

Even though our delivery methods and communication technologies have advanced over our 36 years in business and even though industry knowledge has also advanced, we nevertheless find that our customers and their marketing, manufacturing, and technical employees still require training since manufacturing PET products still requires specialized training and since all companies must deal with employee turnover in their manufacturing operations.

We still offer classroom and laboratory instruction and training as we did initially, but we also now use TV's, smartboards, large format projection, and we offer online presentations when customers can't come to our facilities and laboratories.

Rather than asking one PTI trainer to teach an entire course, we usually ask various PTI experts to teach their own specialties, including materials, blow molding, injection molding, testing, and recycling, and as we added laboratory processing machinery, we moved much of our training from the classroom to the laboratory where students could get real-world hands-on experience.

Sumit Mukherjee training at PTI

Interestingly, and even after 20 years, one of my former customers/students told me that he still remembers seeing a preform blown into free space without a mold (we call that "free blowing") which helped him understand how and why PET preforms inflate to form bottles in a blow mold.

PTI training classes were originally offered only to our Coca-Cola customers since they were manufacturing their own bottles and preforms, but we very quickly learned that the regular turnover of manufacturing and sales personnel at many of our customers meant that regular technical training was needed across the PET industry.

From the beginning, we have offered our standard general PET training course, "Technology and Applications of PET." We offer that course four times each year in the US, and we now also offer that class at PTI-Europe, although we have modified our PTI-Europe training program to fit the specific needs of our European customers. Because both PTI-US and PTI-E have extensive processing and analytical laboratories, our courses today in the US and in Europe include both classroom and hands-on laboratory training.

We have also developed customized training programs for specific customers, and while we offer general training classes where anyone can sign up, we also offer customized programs for specific customers where only a single customer's employees are allowed to sign up; and we offer those customized classes around the world from Asia to South America at our customers' sites, not just at our PTI-US and PTI-E facilities.

Our training courses have even been delivered using "simulation language translation" which is very challenging

Customized training at the customer's site

for both the presenters and the students, but we have proven over many years that even our classes that require language translation are extremely effective.

We have also expanded our course offerings over the years. In addition to PET Technology and Applications (PET 101), we offer more intensive classes on materials, material handling, drying, injection molding, blow molding, testing, and recycling, as well as even more specialized classes which we have prepared for specific customers.

Gary Weaver and Roger Kloepfer training in the Process Laboratory

While we still conduct regular training classes at PTI, we have found that doing training on site at our customers' locations helps to reinforce the material covered in the class because our students are operating their own equipment and working in their own laboratories.

Donald Miller and Tom Carros Training

We have even included a "train the trainer" program so that customers can learn to train their own employees, and several of our customers have asked us to regularly schedule retraining just for their manufacturing and sales personnel, because they know that manufacturing technologies and end-use bottle requirements will keep changing.

One customer has sent employees from each of its manufacturing sites to PTI for training four times each year for the past 16 years!

Because PTI has developed a reputation for providing quality industrial training programs, we have now engaged other industry partners to provide SPE's FastTrack programs and to provide Design of Experiments (DOE) training, where the training includes running actual experiments on injection and blow molding machines.

We did offer an Online Academy for a few years but found that remote live classes better meet the demands of the changing industrial environment.

For the record, PTI has averaged an impressive 12 classes per year over the last 33 years and we have held as many as 45 classes in a single year, just because of demand. At the end of 2021, we estimate that more than 3,000 participants have been trained by PTI since 1986!

PTI Employees Make the Difference

2016 Company Photo

Other key employees who played important roles during the early evolution of PTI and up until today, many of whom are still with PTI, PTI-Europe, and Preform Technologies include Blane Adams, Marcio Amazonas, Yen Andenmatten, Bruce Ankenbrandt, Robin Antoniazza, Tim Apling, Daniel Applegate, Dennis Balduff, Craig Barrow, Barb Balyeat, Julie Barnes, Florence Baroni, Lori Bartman, Jean-Claude Baumgartner, Wes Beebe, Brittanie Begeman, Kara Belcher, Steve Bersinger, Dave Bogstad, Aaron Bolinger, Grant Briggs, Matt Brooks, Leah Broome, Dan Buelow, Scott Bysick, Sherri Carros, Tom Carros, Chip Cereghin, Jan Challen, Kent Challen, Wendy Cone, Spencer Crissman, Bob Cucunato, Loren Curtis, Cassandra Davis, Vickie and Tina Davis, Travis DeHart, Mike Dennis, Pam Douglas, Lori Drown, Christian Ducreux, Ethan Dugan, Laurence Dupraz, Dan Durham, Lou Ann Ervin, Thierry Fabozzi, Antonio Farré, Greg Fisher, Linda Flowers, Kristi Fradette (Cowden), Ron Fradette, Martin Geithmann, Dana Georgerini, Walt Getzinger, Hannah Ginsbach, Jodi Green, Rob Groll, Randy Haar, Denny Hahn, Kim Harbert, Erica Hartman, Jason Haslow, Don Hayward, Steve Hawksworth, Jacob Holcomb, Jim Hull, Alex Hsu, Jim Hussey, Jen Gadient, Roger Kloepfer, Gary Koerner, Lana Komar, Steve Koskie, Christian Kuhl, Ron Kusz, Sarah Laby, Helene Lanctuit, Jérôme Larrieu, Vincent LeGuen, Anita Lemle, Craig Lindsey, Colleen Lockwood, Homer Longoria, Mathieu Larose, Larry Maciolek, Sylvie Magnin, Alison Martin, Carol Matrisciano, Todd Marchal, Bart Mather, Jon McGurk, Steve McNally, Ozzy Medina, Donald Miller, Elaine Miller, Stéphane Morier, Shari Morse, Mitch Mosley, Hassan Mourad, Paramita Mukherjee, Sumit Mukherjee, Joe Nycz, Ray Olinger, Nacho Ortega, Missy Otterson, Aaron Patchett, Craig Peabody, Mark Poddany, Wayne Posey, Ron Puvak, Craig Robinson, Derik Rodriguez, Tana Rogers, Anne Roulin, Jean-Luc Roulin, Chantel Roush, Dave Ryan, Gene Sadzewicz, Pascal Sandoz, Marcia Selleck, Cindy Sheckler, Jim Sheely, Jeff Schellenberg, Henry Schworm, Nicholas Sframeli, Gus Simeo, Danielle Tschappat, Sabrina Taylor, Aaron Teitlebaum, Katerina Toth, William Van Keyenberg, Bill Voyles, Julie Brown Voyles, Tony Waller, Gary Weaver, Vikki Weaver, Jacob Weil, Marty Weishampel, Mike Westmeyer, Julie Wheating, Chris White, Stacey Wilcox, Dan Witham, Keith Wooley, Wei Zhang, Denise Zielinski, and Mike Zielinski.

Dan Durham and Keith Brown

Tracy Momany and Rob Groll

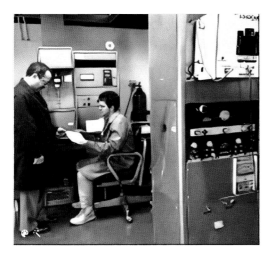

Frank Semersky and Keith Brown

Bob Deardurff and Frank Semersky

Frank Schloss and Scott Steele

Dan Buelow and Vickie Davis

Donald Miller

Craig Peabody

Linda Flowers

Wayne Posey and Roger Kleopfer

Aaron Bolinger

Jason Haslow, Steve Bersinger, Wayne Posey,
Steve Koskie, Daniel Applegate

Green (100% RPET) Bottle Production for a
Lucas County recycling promotion

The Analytical Testing Laboratory

Aaron Bollinger, Daniel Applegate and Chris White
(speaking) with students

Barb Balyeat

Daniel Applegate

Julie Brown Voyles

Kara Belcher

Sumit Mukherjee

Brittanie Begeman and Anita Lemle

End of the Year PTI Service Awards Celebration

Front - Kara Belcher, Wendy Cone, Anita Lemle, 2nd - Lori Drown, Greg Fisher, Vickie Davis, Jodi Green, 3rd - Keith Brown, Loren Curtis, Jen Gadient, Elaine Miller, Carol Matrisciano, Keith Wooley, 4th - Ethan Dugan, Ron Fradette, Cindy Sheckler

"A Great Place to Work"

Frank Schloss, Tom Brady, Henry Schworm

Dan Durham, Oliver Brownridge

Denise and Mike Zielinski

*Chantel Roush, Kristy Fradette, Tina Davis,
Jodi Green, Vickie Davis, Anita Ort*

Tracy and Todd Momany

Vikki Weaver

Steve and Jenny Koskie

Tom Brady and Thierry Fabozzi

Betsy Brady, Ron Puvak, Nicole and Jon McGurk,
Anna and Spencer Crissman

Missy Otterson, Elaine Miller, Wayne Posey,
Pam Douglas

Julie Wheating

Barb Balyeat, Elaine Miller, Tracy Momany, Lana
Komar, Lori Bartman

Tana Rogers, Lou Ervin, Julie Wheating

Don and Mary Jane Hayward

Nancy and Joe Nycz and Rob and Lori Groll

Gary and Diane Koerner and Lori and Jeff Yoder

Dennis Balduff and Shari Morse

Mary Jo and Don Hayward, Bob and Sue Deardurff

Dan and Joan Durham

Sumit and Paramita Mukherjee

Terry Lee and Dan Buelow

Tom and Sherry Carros

Tom Brady and Alison Martin

78

Missy Otterson and Tom Brady

Lori and Rob Groll

Julie and Keith Brown

Ron and Diane Ley

Al and Trudy Uhlig, Marilee and Tim Spann

Don Hayward, Bill Pratt, Brian Klausing

Summer picnic at the Carson Pool

Company Volleyball Game

Pam and Jack Ritchie, Shari Morse

*Sue and Bob Deardurff, Mary Jane and Don Hayward,
Jack and Pam Ritchie*

Craig and Missy Otterson, Denise Zielinski, Gary Weaver

Summer party for PTI families

Marty Geithmann, Scott Steele, Don Hayward, Bob Deardurff

10-year awards for Betsy, Bob, and Marilee

Jean Bina, Dennis and Denise Balduff

Lori and Bill Bartman

Tom with Denise, Marilee, Diane, and Rachel

Matt and Chantel Walters, Vickie and Paul Davis

Allena and Oliver Brownridge

Gary and Diane Koerner, and Cindy and Walt Getzinger

Dan Durham, PVS Prasad, Scott Steele, William Van Keyenberg, Lori Carson, Donald Miller, Jon McGurk, Pamela Douglas, Tracy Momany, Ron Puvak, Sumit Mukherjee, Marcio Amazonas, Thierry Fabozzi at the NPE 2012

Tom and Betsy Brady

Marcia and Gary Selleck, Long Fei and Tommie Chang

Alison and Drew Rogers

Betsy Brady and Gary Weaver

Mike Zielinski

Denise and Eugene Sadzewicz, Bill and Ruth Voyles

Julie Wheating, Tana Rogers, Julie Barnes

Henry Schworm, Julie and Keith Brown

PTI Musicians

Michael and Pam Douglas

Todd and Tracy Momany and Marcia and Gary Selleck

2012 PTI Senior Management Team

Frank Schloss, Jim Sheely, Scott Steele, Thierry Fabozzi, Donald Miller
Seated: Tracy Momany, Tom Brady, Betsy Brady

Rob Groll speaking at a PTI Christmas Party

Tom's Annual Christmas Party Speech

Scott Steele and Betsy and Tom Brady

Jim Sheely Retiring

Chantel Walters, Elaine Miller, Craig Barrow, Pam Douglas

The original team celebrating Year 20

Year-end service awards

Year-end service awards

Free party entertainment

Party on!

Ribbon-cutting at Phoenix Technologies

Alliance between UT and PTI and Phoenix Technologies

Jack Ritchie, Jean Bina, Scott Steele, Marty Geithmann

Tana Rogers and Matt Brooks

2000 Halloween Party

2000 PTI Company Picture

2012 Plastics Packaging Hall of Fame Banquet

Sumit Mukherjee, Marcio Amazonas, Pam Douglas, Dan Durham, Tracy Momany
Betsy and Tom Brady, Amy and Scott Steel, John Maddox

2013 Company Picture

New (PET Technology) Business Development

As PTI continued to grow and to provide technical development services to virtually all companies involved in PET packaging including brand owners, converters, resin suppliers, machinery manufacturers and raw material suppliers, PTI professionals developed several exciting and high potential technologies which were owned by PTI, and which offered potential sales or licensing opportunities.

To take advantage of these proprietary technologies, PTI created a New Business Development activity having the charter to pursue internal technology developments as business opportunities, either by joint venture, by licensing, or by creating independent companies.

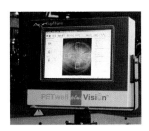

In 2001 PTI identified Non-Contact International (NCI) as a joint venture partner with the goal of developing a commercial prototype for an on-line bottle wall thickness measurement technology developed and patented by PTI. The joint venture partners formed a separate licensing company, PETWall LLC, which completed the development of the wall thickness gauge and licensed the technology to a global supplier of on-line inspection equipment, Agr-TopWave.

Today, Agr-TopWave manufactures, sells, and services online plastic bottle inspection equipment, trade-named **PETWall Vision™** which utilizes the original **PETWall™** wall thickness gauging systems technology.

Those early relationships between PTI and its partners spurred the development of additional instrumentation products, including **TorqTraQ™**, a hand-held closure removal torque meter, **WallTraQ™**, a wall thickness gauge, **VacTraQ™**, a vacuum resistance meter, and **OxyTraQ™**, an oxygen permeation system which was licensed to MOCON for manufacture and sale as another instrument in the MOCON product line.

TorqTraQ™   *WallTraQ™*   *VacTraQ™*   *OxyTraQ™*

In 2003 PTI formed a joint venture with Container Consulting Inc. (CCI) for the purpose of commercializing and licensing another PTI proprietary technology, **Virtual Prototyping (VP)™**. **VP™** is a computer simulation of PET preform/bottle design and processing which allows the user to optimize the design of a preform and bottle combination prior to prototyping. **VP™** simulates the reheat-blow molding process using a computer-designed preform and then iterating the initial preform design by predicting the final bottle material distribution and performance. This very powerful **VP™** software offers the industry higher speed and accuracy for routine bottle design and development and is now available for license from either CCI or from PTI.

oPTI™ foamed PET technology was developed and patented by PTI, but a partnership with Ferromatik/Milacron (injection machines) and Foboha (injection molds) was essential to develop the needed commercial overmolding system. This unique and proprietary technology was featured at NPE and then transferred to Preform Technologies where production samples were made for customers. Coca-Cola successfully test-marketed the technology in Europe, but it was never introduced in the US because of cost.

Other technologies developed by PTI include the **NFA Leak Monitor™**, a bottle imperfection detector which uses an ultrasonic method to "hear" defects as they are created during the blow molding process, a **Laser Measurement System (LMS™)** which automatically creates a complete map of the outer dimensions of a bottle using laser detection of the outside surface in three-dimensional space, and the **PED-2000™**, a preform "free-blow" device for the laboratory which allows the user to quickly and accurately determine "natural stretch ratio" for any bottle-making resin.

PTI built and sold these internally developed electronic systems as PTI products, but we also licensed the **NFA Leak Monitor™** to **ALPS Inspection**, a **TSAI** company that manufactures and sells in-line leak detection systems to the packaging industry (https://www.alpsleak.com).

PTI from 2008-2011

This story is courtesy of Mr. Craig Barrow, PTI CEO from 2008-2011

Craig Barrow

In late 2007 I was finishing up a hedge fund turnaround engagement working in Indiana as Chief Financial Officer and Executive Vice President of Sales and Marketing. While having dinner with Frank Semersky, a longtime friend and former O-I co-worker, I mentioned that my mission in Indiana was wrapping up so I was about to take on another turnaround assignment that would involve more nights on the road. Since my children were still young and my father was aging, I told Frank that something closer to home would be very appealing. Frank said there might be an opportunity for me to join him at Plastic Technologies, Inc.

Frank Semersky

I was somewhat familiar with PTI, given my history at Owens-Illinois and my relationship with Frank, so I was excited about the opportunity to learn more about the company, the players, and the "go forward" plans. I met with Tom and Betsy Brady who were Founder/President and Chief Financial Officer respectively. The opportunity they described was very intriguing. They were looking for someone with broad business experience to work with the management team to forge a transition plan for PTI to position this wildly successful company for the next 25 years.

I accepted the role of Vice President and Chief Operating Officer early in 2008, and it became immediately apparent that the PTI family of companies was very complex. The company embraced the entrepreneurial spirit of the founder and combined that with the creativity of the management team so there were many moving parts as work shifted between the various companies. My first six months were spent attending senior staff meetings and internal strategy sessions, and meeting with customers. I tried to absorb the impressive culture of the company and the mix of talents and personalities that made it all work.

PTI had been successful in hiring bright young engineering interns who got real-world work experience while being paid and while auditioning for long term positions in a very creative and challenging environment. PTI also had thrived in its role as an industry thought leader, but as the PET industry matured, other challenges and competitors began to emerge which included the fact that many of PTI's packaging customers and their vendors sought to expand their own services and capabilities and thus began to compete with services that previously had been virtually proprietary to PTI. So, what were my ideas about the executable strategies to position PTI moving forward?

PTI Strategies

- **Drive Revenue:** Solidify and build on existing customer relationships with a focused sales approach to grow revenue as efficiently as possible.
- **Enable Accountability:** Empower the department leaders with technology to enable them to be accountable for their work to ensure projects were proposed and executed profitably.
- **Enter New Markets:** Expand the PTI brand into new areas both technologically and geographically.

Driving Revenue

PTI had been very successful building the business using a traditional entrepreneurial model. Engineers would network within client companies, and this would generate a steady source of new projects. This resulted in excellent growth and a list of impressive clients. Over the years, however, clients were taking more work "in house" so PTI's role in some projects began to diminish and numerous projects resulted in PTI providing expert training for customer in-house resources.

The other reality was that networking with other engineers who were often mid-level employees did not give access to more strategic projects like those that initially launched PTI. Strategic projects were identified and managed by PTI leadership and the PTI network.

Jim Sheely

Ron Puvak

Marcio Amazonas

It seemed that a more structured approach to selling would be beneficial both near term and long term for PTI. I felt that bringing in a VP Sales caliber person would help in this regard, and I hired James Sheely to join the team. Jim had been a successful executive sales leader and could assist in this effort by helping us create and roll out more sales structure and by leading by example with large complex clients. Jim's experience with Monroe Mold and Die enabled him to understand many of the engineering complexities of various projects, to leverage his sales skills, and to negotiate and close deals. Ron Puvak, then Director of Marketing, was also tapped to assist based on his effort and great success with "The Packaging Conference" while working with Frank Semersky. We also hired Marcio Amazonas who was based in Atlanta, had strong ties from previously working with Coca-Cola, who spoke Spanish fluently because he grew up in Brazil, and who worked with Jim Sheely and Dan Durham to focus on Colgate Palmolive and Coca-Cola respectively at a strategic level while our engineers continued to support them and to sell additional projects.

We also began to pursue business with new customers like PepsiCo who, given our long and successful history with Coca-Cola, PTI had previously avoided, but times were changing everywhere, and Coke was building more and more internal capabilities. During this time PTI innovated several new technologies including the Mucell™ foamed PET container which we trademarked oPTI™ and we pursued Proctor and Gamble as a potential customer for this technology.

oPTI™, Deep Grip, and Novelty Containers

While finding a proper point of contact in a multi-billion-dollar company proved to be a challenge, when I saw that the Vice President of P&G's New Product Development was going to be a featured speaker at a conference in Florida, I flew to the conference and sought her out at the social function, specifically to explore P&G's possible interest in this new technology. As a result of that conversation, we did carry out numerous projects with P&G over several years, and with several other customers who wished to explore the use of the oPTI™ technology. Unfortunately, as compelling as the oPTI™ technology was from a marketing perspective, customers never commercialized oPTI™, because there was an added cost.

We were also challenged by the success of our Preform Technologies' (PTLLC) business that was rapidly running out of space and because we also required some additional capital for machine repairs and upgrades to grow the business. I hired Stephen Hawksworth, a global business consultant and former associate in various business ventures, who was given PTLLC as one of his first projects to analyze. Steve ran various scenarios as part of his analysis and wrote a compelling proposal for additional investment in PTLLC which was presented to the PTLLC Board of Directors. The proposed investment involved securing more space and adding capacity to our equipment. Steve successfully located a nearby facility and negotiated a lease agreement that provided space for current production and the option to expand as the business grew.

From there, Jim Sheely was charged with leading PTLLC, a business that required a close working relationship with Colgate Palmolive and other customers that Jim had cultivated along the way. The early PTLLC success story is found elsewhere in this book, but more recent revenue growth from Preform Technologies was the result of Jim executing and building on the analysis and recommendations of Steve.

Enabling Accountability

PTI was very fortunate to have a very capable couple who started the company and managed its early growth. Dr. Tom and Betsy Brady each had a role, with Tom as Founder and CEO and Betsy as Chief Financial Officer (among other duties). Betsy managed the various PTI businesses finances for many years from her desktop computer and distributed monthly performance reports to the Executive Staff for review and discussion. By this time, however, computer driven capabilities had evolved tremendously and were increasingly available to small businesses. It was time to move from the traditional command and control approach to a distributed operating model that would add efficiency, streamline processes, and give our various department vice presidents more autonomy. We implemented NetSuite for this purpose.

Each department could now track its proposals and projects, as well as more traditional engineering services productivity metrics such as staff utilization. The flexible nature of the NetSuite product made it a good choice and NetSuite could accommodate the kind of growth PTI had experienced while also providing an option for better management of the existing PTI family of companies and for identifying and creating additional future PTI family companies.

Entering New Markets

Exploring new markets for PTI's services was a logical way to leverage the company brand and its global customer network of connections. Frank Semersky had already started PTI-Europe SARL in Yverdon-les Bains, Switzerland but the most promising new growth markets seemed to be in the BRIC countries (Brazil, Russia, India & China), although we ruled out both Russia and China and focused on exploring only Brazil and India.

Marcio Amazonas and I travelled to São Paulo to visit Coca-Cola Brazil and to explore establishing a beach head there. While it was an illuminating visit, the challenges of doing business in Brazil were enormous.

Next, we scheduled a trip to India to meet with several existing customers as well as to meet with prospective partners, with the idea of doing lab work along with our partners at Mocon, Inc. Meetings with Colgate Palmolive, Coke, and others, including a visit with Reckitt Benckiser, a large multinational consumer goods company we had never done business with, were on the agenda. Clearly, India was an enormous growth opportunity since Coke told us that only 2% of all beverages were at that time consumed from a container. Coke said that as the middle class in India grew exponentially, so too would the demand for beverages in low-cost containers. We made several good contacts in India which gave PTI a foothold in India that was consummated after my time as president.

Also, about this time, Saudi Arabia was looking to create a "plastics city" where any plastics industry company could locate. I accompanied Steve Hawksworth (fluent in Arabic) to Riyadh to spend a week learning what the Saudis were planning and to explore where PTI might fit. We visited King Faud University, the Royal Saudi Commissioners, and the training facilities and proposed site of the "plastics city." There was no shortage of well-trained engineers or capital, but we learned that women were not allowed in the workplace and PTI had many women employees in both engineering and management positions. We explained this to the Saudis who graciously acknowledged that this cultural issue would have to be addressed, but they also said that "culture change is a slow process in Saudi Arabia."

One of the last initiatives under the "Entering New Markets" category was our investigation of the potential for a merger with one of the major players in the PET container business and we considered the possibility of either a vertical or horizontal industry merger. Toward that end I broached the subject with Husky Injection Molding Systems, in Canada. They showed interest in the idea which I reported back to PTI Management, and which teed up the idea that moved forward from there.

I left PTI in October of 2011 feeling as though we had made substantial progress in positioning Plastic Technologies Inc. for the next 25 years.

PS. As Founder of PTI and as the author of this history of PTI, I want to express my sincere thanks and gratitude to Craig for taking on the challenge of redirecting our entrepreneurial business at a time when redirection was very much needed, as is true for virtually every startup after a few years. PTI would not be where it is today without Craig Barrow's professional business guidance during those transitional years - Tom Brady

PTI from 2013 to 2017

This story is courtesy of Mr. Scott Steele, PTI Founder, Owner, and President and Chief Operating Officer from 2013 to 2017

Scott and Amy Steele

As one of the founding PTI employees (Tom's words, not mine), I took over as President in early 2013. The business climate was difficult at the time, but the company was well positioned for renewed success based on several emerging opportunities generated in the preceding years. While I was hired as President and Chief Operating Officer, I implemented a new organizational approach which recognized the role Betsy Brady had been quietly fulfilling throughout her PTI years. I managed sales and operations and Betsy managed the financial and administrative side of the business.

Early in my tenure, Jim Sheely was reassigned to exclusively focus on managing Preform Technologies LLC (PTLLC). Jim had been assisting with business development for PTI as well as managing the new business opportunities for PTLLC. After Jim was confirmed as the president of PTLLC and once he had focused his full energy on running PTLLC, a financial turnaround followed. However, a tough situation quickly developed when Jim's wife Rita had a reversal in her long battle with health issues. Fortunately, Jim somehow managed to assume his new expanded role at PTLLC while still simultaneously dealing with his teenage

PTI Family of Companies Management Team
Frank Schloss, Jim Sheely, Scott Steele, Thierry Fabozzi, Donald Miller, Tracy Momany, Tom Brady, Betsy Brady

children at a time of great personal loss. To Jim's credit, he persevered, and PTLLC turned the corner to become profitable while beginning to pay down the debt that had accumulated over several years.

Tervis Tumblers

An early success at PTLLC was the relationship Jim developed with Tervis, Inc. (www.tervis.com) in Florida. PTI designed a blow molded 24-ounce tumbler with a new dispensing feature for Tervis. The tumbler was one of the first blow molded applications using Eastman Chemical's new Tritan™ copolyester resin and became one of Tervis' best-selling products. PTLLC began immediate commercial production using PTI's single cavity system but quickly transitioned to two-cavity molds and rebuilt three well-used Nissei machines to support the growing business. The expanded PTLLC business required a significant effort by PTI's Tooling Services Group and by the PTI Analytical Lab, as well as the relentless efforts of the PTLLC staff. However, a very challenging welding quality problem between the inside and outside tumbler components was noted in the field which, along with the typical challenges of commercializing a new product, made for a difficult first year. Nevertheless, the two-piece tumbler took off in the market for Tervis and ultimately became the key to helping PTLLC grow its business.

Frank Semersky

Early in my tenure, a huge void at PTI was created when Frank Semersky retired. Frank was not only a key business development person for PTI, but he was the force behind many of PTI's most successful product and business innovations. Frank's mind was constantly inventing new approaches which stimulated everyone at PTI to think more creatively. PETWall™ Profiler, a non-contact thickness gauging device, TorqTraq™, a handheld device for measuring closure torque removal, LMS™, a lab device for measuring bottle dimensions, and oPTI™ foamed PET containers all had Frank's fingerprints on them. PTI leadership had worked very hard over the years to create a culture where any employee could propose commercializable ideas, which led to PTI's focus on innovation and eventually to the annual selection of PTI's "Innovator of the Year" which helped propel PTI's reputation as an industry thought leader.

One of the management innovations that I and my senior staff implemented was the creation of an innovation team which solicited and managed creative ideas that were proposed by employees from any of the PTI companies. Quarterly innovation awards were presented, which led to naming the Innovator of the Year at annual year-end holiday parties. Frank Schloss was selected as the first PTI Innovator of the Year in 2014 for his idea to combine Radco's Infusion Technology with oPTI™ technology to make an opaque colored PET bottle that could be recycled into clear PET. Lori Bartman received the award in 2015 when she helped a major client develop a novel hot fill package and Aaron Bollinger was selected in 2016 for his work on feedback process control of the blow molding process. Appropriately, the Innovators received their awards under a "Light Bulb," the symbol of all bright ideas!

PTI Innovation Team
Jon McGurk, Aaron Teitlebaum, Linda Flowers,
Spencer Crissman, Frank Semersky, Ron Puvak

Aaron Bollinger and Steve Koskie

Jason Haslow

Marty Geithmann

Jon McGurk and Gary Weaver

The four years of my tenure as President and COO also saw the retirement of several senior scientists, engineers, technicians, and managers, including Frank Schloss, Don Hayward, Denise Zielinski, Dennis Balduff, Mike Tucholski, Walt Getzinger, Bart Mather, Ron Fradette, and Bob Deardurff, all long-time and experienced employees. The history of PTI would not be complete without some mention of their more notable contributions.

Dennis Balduff, Scott Steele, Frank Schloss

Dennis and Denise Balduff.
Mary Jane and Don Hayward

Marty Geithmann, Scott Steele,
Don Hayward, Bob Deardurff

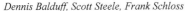

Tom Brady & Frank Schloss

Frank Schloss was PTI's materials expert who was willing to investigate the correct way to measure almost any plastic property. Frank willingly accepted the role of managing all Phoenix Technologies' food grade RPET FDA submissions and it took someone with Frank's patience and demeanor to persevere when testing and submissions bogged down. PTI engineers and management were always frustrated that approvals did not happen faster, and Frank bore the brunt of much of that unnecessary internal pressure. However, he not only managed the internal pressure that resulted from waiting for government to respond to our regulatory applications, but I can't recall any PTI regulatory application which was not eventually approved, because of Frank's diligence. Managing PTI customer expectations, as well as soliciting responses from several of PTI's less attentive service vendors, while at the same time keeping peace internally among PTI scientists and engineers, was something that only Frank could do, and which eventually led to successful FDA submissions.

Gary Landis and Frank Schloss

Frank was also an industry expert on recyclability, and he created one of the only recycling laboratories in the industry at PTI, specifically to demonstrate the viability of new packaging materials and innovations.

His pioneering work with industry trade groups resulted in a test regimen that is still recognized and used today as the industry standard for evaluating new packaging technologies for their impact on recyclability.

97

Don Hayward also retired from PTI after leading Phoenix Technologies as its General Manager. Don started up the very first Phoenix recycling line and negotiated approval from Phoenix's first customer, Colgate Palmolive. Don was a unique talent and a person everyone liked to be around. He was witty as well as brilliant. At six foot eight, he was also the player we wanted on our PTI intramural teams!

Don was the primary architect of the newly created Phoenix Technologies recycling business, and it was Don who specified all the primary equipment that Phoenix ran during the first several years of production. At the very beginning when Colgate asked PTI to supply the first recycled PET in the industry for their Palmolive detergent bottles, only one extrusion line was required which included a 3-inch used extruder, several used dryers, and a myriad of other parts that Don and Bob Deardurff used to create our first commercial system.

Jack Ritchie, Bob Deardurff, Dennis Balduff, Don Hayward, and Tom Brady

Colgate was so pleased that they soon asked to purchase even more recycled PET and it was Don, supported by Bob Deardurff, who made the decision to scrap the used equipment and to buy all new equipment from leading suppliers. Not all of Don's PTI peers supported that decision but it turned out to be the right thing to do. Don and the Phoenix team quickly scaled the operation to 3 lines and delivered quality RPET from the very beginning. Doing it right, and not just making do, taught all of us a valuable lesson.

The first recycled PET that Phoenix Technologies supplied to Colgate was nonfood grade, but the industry's desire for food and beverage applications was strong too, so Don led the development of the patented Phoenix Process™ which allowed Phoenix Technologies to manufacture food grade RPET LNOp™ pellets and LNOc™ flake for Coca-Cola and other brand owners. Don was an inventor and concluded his career as a scientist at PTI while trying to invent a sensing technique for measuring crystallinity in PET which showed promise in the laboratory, but we eventually did not have the resources to perfect and commercialize the technology.

Dennis Balduff also retired from PTI, but Dennis was on constant loan to Phoenix and was involved in many of Phoenix's commercial engineering successes. Dennis settled back into the PTI Materials Group in 2011 and finished his career at PTI while helping to develop and commercialize the CyclePET™ process which resulted in FDA letters of no-objection (LNOs) for Phoenix Technologies' food grade RPET and the eventual licensing of the CyclePET™ process to Coca-Cola. Dennis also helped generate all the data from various experiments to support all of Phoenix's submissions to FDA.

Dennis Balduff

At PTI, Dennis and Frank Schloss together built the recycled plastics laboratory, including a wash tank, a rotary vacuum dryer, and twin-screw extruders, and they kept the lab running and full of business. They also resurrected a T R Long axial stretching machine that was used to characterize the strain hardening behavior of new polymers and several bio polymers. Dennis was an able scientist who not only ran experiments but who also was able to interpret results. Any time new equipment was installed in one of the PTI labs, Dennis was there to learn about that equipment and to make it operational.

PTI Recycling Laboratory

Pam Douglas, Elaine Miller, Julie Brown, Frank Schloss, Missy Otterson, Lori Yoder, Denise, Zielinski

Denise Salmon Zielinski was another employee whose tenure dated back to the early PTI days at 333 14th street. Like many of the original core PTI employees, founders, and owners, Denise always wore several hats. She was hired as an administrative assistant but quickly assumed multiple roles to fill the many gaps. For many years all PTI travel was booked by Denise who became an in-house travel agent. All PTI's constantly travelling engineers' flights and hotels were booked by Denise while the travel agency printed the tickets. Denise also took on the role of booking outside laboratory testing, and it was Denise who organized and administered PTI's testing schedules through the PTI scheduling system.

However, Denise's role as lab coordinator might have been her most important contribution. Originally, the Analytical Lab (ALab) would occasionally receive requests for basic testing, such as for AA, IV etc., where the testing was not connected to a customer's technical development project. Sometimes these requests came directly from PTI customers and sometimes from word-of-mouth references to PTI's testing laboratory. In the early days, these requests were handled by a committee, which was not very efficient. Denise, however, made it a priority to maintain direct contact with all PTI customers and to get their testing scheduled. Then, she would diligently follow up to make sure that

Denise Zielinski

customers' samples were ready, testing was completed, data was checked for correctness and accuracy, and that data was reported promptly to the customer. Because of Denise's diligent supervision and rapid response to clients, PTI revenue from testing services grew substantially, especially once the industry learned to contact Denise directly.

Walt and Cindy Getzinger

Walt Getzinger, Bart Mather, and Mike Tucholski all worked in the PTI Processing Laboratory for many years. Walt was one of the Kloster Company employees who helped PTI move from 14th Street downtown to Wolf Creek Executive Park and who then joined PTI as a full-time employee back in 1993. He quickly became an expert injection molding technician and was key to building PTI's very successful Plastics Processing Laboratory (PLab). Walt not only learned to operate every one of PTI's PLab machines, but he also taught machine operation training classes and supervised PTI's laboratory injection processing operations for many years.

Bart Mather, Mike Tucholski, and Ron Fradette joined PTI as experienced lab technicians a few years after Walt and they also became experienced and essential plastic processing laboratory technicians. Walt and the other PLab technicians all spent time with customers in the PLab and helped those same customers to install and to learn to process on equipment in the customers' plants.

One of PTI's keys to success was that PTI's PLab technicians were not only known for their combination of molding and testing skills but they were also personable and front-line salespeople for PTI. Customers that visited PTI's PLab and ALab universally enjoyed working side by side with PTI's laboratory technicians.

Sue and Bob Deardurff

Before he retired from Phoenix, Bob Deardurff formally retired from PTI. At his 30th PTI anniversary the following words were written by me on behalf of Bob's PTI colleagues.

"It is well known here at PTI that Bob was the first employee that Tom hired. I think all of us who have followed Bob know that he paved the way for many of us to find our own pathway at PTI, including me, Scott Steele. It was Bob who reached out to me when I elected to leave my job with the big company to join PTI. Bob was already working with Western Container, Southeastern Container, and Apple Container and he had even negotiated a second contract to provide regular processing support for those early customers.

As was often true in those early days, I'm sure Bob was asked by Dick Roswech or John Bombace whether we really could make happen what we said we could and, of course, Bob responded affirmatively, on behalf of PTI. However, I think I can say with some confidence that after his first trip to Southeastern Container, Bob returned home wondering how we could ever deal with all the issues and opportunities that he saw in the Southeastern plant!

Regardless of the extensive experience we all had with PET processing equipment, we for sure did not know everything that was required to address Southeastern's needs during those years. But we did understand the fundamental materials science behind the plastics manufacturing processes in the field and, more importantly, we were very good at building our knowledge base by mentally connecting the science of plastics processing to the results of our experimental efforts. As a result, we made every project a learning opportunity.

Bob was also the first PTI employee to sell a PTI Technical Service Agreement to a customer. He designed and sold that first agreement to an Italian closure supplier named Nocera Umbra who, if you can believe it, agreed to pay us a year in advance.... and Nocera Umbra seldom asked questions about invoicing. In fact, our early experience with Nocera Umbra helped us learn how to become better plastics industry consultants.

That first call from Colgate Palmolive, our first major US customer opportunity other than Coca-Cola, went to Tom. But it was Bob and I who travelled to Cambridge Ohio and told Dennis Calabro we could help him, even though we had little experience with non-round containers or with liquid soap or with the Cincinnati Milacron machines they were running at the time. It was also Bob who recognized the opportunity to supply Colgate with melt-filtered pelletized recycled PET (RPET) before Colgate even knew they needed or could use RPET. In fact, it was Bob who sold Colgate on the idea that we could design and install and run a first-of-its-kind RPET processing plant; and it was Bob who suggested that we would sell that plant to Colgate when it was proven, if Colgate decided that they wanted to own their own RPET processing plant. Of course, we worked hard to make sure that we operated that first Phoenix plant so efficiently that Colgate would never ask to purchase it and, as they say, the rest is history! Within a matter of only a few years, Phoenix Technologies grew to become the largest producer of food-grade recycled PET in the country.

Under Bob's continued leadership Phoenix experienced many firsts, including earning the first FDA-approval for making food grade recycled PET resin from curbside-collected bottles; previous approvals were for recycled PET made only from deposit state bottles. Phoenix was also the first plastic recycler to petition for and obtain FDA approval to use recycled PET containers that had contained all food types, and to use Phoenix recycled PET in microwave food contact applications, well ahead of the industry.

Bob is also recognized for his community involvement and is a long-time supporter and huge proponent of the Sunshine Children's home here in Toledo."

Scott Steele on behalf of PTI Friends of Bob Deardurff, 2016

The sales void created when Frank Semersky retired was a constant focus of attention. During my years as President and COO, strategic planning involved managing the decline of PTI's business volume, but also involved creating and establishing a new sales and business model. During these years, PTI attempted to rework the sales function several times, but I was always reminded that the key to PTI's early sales success had been that everyone in the organization participated in sales. This included laboratory staff as well as our engineers. PLab Manager, Tom Carros, constantly informed visitors of other PTI services and ALab Manager, Keith Brown, also asked customers questions about what else they might need. The CAD department was also positioned to contribute to sales, as were all PTI project engineers, which is what I tried to build upon during my years as president.

"Everyone sells" became our mantra during my years as President, which was my approach to decentralizing sales. We created sales teams that were focused on the most important clients and hired sales representatives for our most important new markets. We also increased spending on trade shows, created outbound marketing materials, and added several new dedicated salespeople. Whether the market turned or whether we just didn't execute our sales strategies well enough is no longer relevant, but the facts are that during this several year period, the growth of PTI stalled, which mandated several painful layoffs as we reduced our permanent staff from nearly 100 to 60. Layoffs and low morale, unfortunately but understandably, also caused several high potential young employees to leave PTI.

Nevertheless, it is worth celebrating the fact that during this very difficult time for all of industry, PTI did experience several successes that helped position PTI for the future. The materials group maintained strong relationships with plastic resin and additive suppliers as those suppliers generally cut back on their own internal R&D, which helped to assure steady business for PTI's laboratories. Also, while most of PTI's traditional customers had learned a great deal themselves about developing PET packaging, over time, those same customers were paring back their internal R&D resources, which also helped generate a reasonably steady flow of R&D requests from customers who concluded that they could reduce their total R&D expenses by contracting work out to PTI.

During this time, the Materials Group obtained take-or-pay contracts with two major resin suppliers to provide commercial materials development support, because those resin companies still needed access to production molding machines without breaking into their own production schedules.

The Materials Group also created and advertised a new service to characterize resin formulations while requiring as little as one pound of test resin, which proved to be an important service for customers who were experimenting with new biomaterials. This new service became a key to keeping both the ALab and the PLab profitable during those tough years of business transition.

It should also be noted that we continued to enjoy excellent relationships with our historically key significant clients, including Southeastern Container, a Coca-Cola Cooperative that continued to pursue new opportunities vigorously, and with Colgate Palmolive which also continued to innovate with new package designs and to "light weight" their then-current packaging to encourage consumer "sustainability."

PTI also engaged in several interesting new plastic aerosol container development projects, and the industry drive for more sustainability caused the beverage industry to introduce bio-derived PET during this time. The introduction of bio-derived PET resulted in a significant uptick in PTI's materials development and testing business, although this did not lead to increased package development work at PTI since bio-derived PETs were essentially synthetic PET compositions and were "drop-in" replacements for oil-based PET package and preform designs.

Nevertheless, the new urgency for developing bio-derived plastics like PHA and PGA was just beginning, and PTI was able to play a valuable role in this emerging industry activity since PTI had all the required testing and prototyping capabilities already in place.

Thierry Fabozzi

Another important PTI evolution during this transitional time was the attraction and hiring of Thierry Fabozzi to run PTI-Europe. Thierry had worked for Nestle, a PTI-Europe customer, and came to PTI as an injection molding and blow molding subject matter expert. He also brought new skills and experience involving the development and commercialization of thin wall packaging which was just emerging as a preferred single serve packaging option.

oPTI™ Container and Preform

Thierry was also able to leverage his prior experience with Milacron to design and build an over-molding system capable of running PTI's oPTI™ technology which PTI was actively trying to license. By partnering with Milacron and Foboha, we were able to create and install a state-of-the-art cube molding system at Preform Technologies LLC. Our 4-cavity over-molding system made its debut at the 2017 K-Show in Dusseldorf which resulted in several high-profile press releases announcing the partnership between our companies. Unfortunately, while the major brand owners all loved the appearance of oPTI™, we could not convince the brand owners to commit to a market introduction, likely because those brand owners were also struggling with the same global economic recession that we were dealing with here in the US.

Nevertheless, in hindsight, the entire effort was well worth the increased press coverage because PTI's brand recognition increased significantly from the oPTI™ near-commercial experience, and the oPTI™ experience also marked the transitioning of PTLLC from the use of well-used and well-worn equipment to investing in new processing machines which were required to grow the business.

Ron Puvak

Another significant development during this time was that PTI's marketing and sales team, led by Ron Puvak, helped PTI create an important relationship with Mocon, a supplier of proprietary permeability testing equipment. Mocon had licensed PTI's OxyTraq™ transport testing technology several years earlier, but Mocon also provided permeability testing services to the industry, so Mocon was also a direct competitor for PTI's oxygen and gas permeation testing. However, Ron and our entire marketing team continued to build a relationship with Mocon that turned Mocon into more of a strategic partner than a competitor. In fact, new state-of-the-art Mocon permeation equipment was placed in our PTI-Europe ALab, and we reached an agreement with Mocon to use Mocon's European sales system to pursue work together. PTI and Mocon even shared booth space at the primary European trade shows.

Despite this collaborative relationship with Mocon, however, permeation work in Europe generally also dropped off during this period which unfortunately meant that even this new partnership relationship with Mocon did not result in any significant increase in testing activity in. Europe.

The Mocon relationship did, however, lead PTI to an important opportunity in India when a Mocon agent in India introduced us to a company named Hemetek which was also running a successful testing business. The Hemetek business model was to sell testing services that could lead to instrument sales, but because several of Hemetek's testing customers could not afford the rather expensive western prices for testing instrumentation, those customers continued to have Hemetek run the required tests.

Announcing the Hemetec-PTI Agreement

The PTI/Hemetek relationship began with PTI supplying its well-recognized PET Technology training programs, which allowed PTI to introduce Hemetek to PTI customers. Eventually, those same customers convinced us to put in a bottle testing lab in India, which we did as a joint venture with Hemetec. Greg Fisher, Director of PTI's Global Testing and Analytical Laboratory Services, was responsible for training and qualifying a lab halfway around the world and did a remarkable job. The lab gained ISO certification, a first for PTI, which gave PTI a presence in the important growing Indian market.

During these several years, another local Northwest Ohio company, Radco, also introduced PTI to a technology that had great potential. Radco had designed and built an automated bread making machine and had obtained the rights to a technology which infused colors into plastics.

An earlier PTI innovation was the development of a novel chemical approach to create colored plastics that could be separated out during the recycling process, but Radco's technology offered the potential to color just the surface of the container material which allowed the colorant to be removed using mild chemicals during the recycling process.

While the idea did work as advertised in the laboratory, it proved too difficult to achieve effective color removal at scale, so PTI abandoned the commercialization of this technology for packaging.

In retrospect, there was no shortage of new and innovative ideas during these years, but low industry profitability limited the willingness of most companies to attempt new approaches.

PreTemp™ Instrument

Nevertheless, the PTI Instrument Group, led by Donald Miller, invented a PreTemp™ temperature probe that could quickly measure the inside wall temperature distribution of a heated preform. When we discovered that a group in Europe had an interfering patent, rather than risk a legal dispute, we elected to license the patent from Blow Molding Technologies in Belfast, Ireland which resulted in the opportunity for PTI to sell PreTemp™ probes profitably to new and existing customers.

TorqTraQ™ sales also remained strong during this time and the sale of PTI instruments generally was a key to helping keep the PTI enterprise moving creatively during these challenging times.

PTI's Tooling Services Group also entered into an exclusive agreement to license quick-change Nissei machine tooling technology from Big Three Precision, a leading local mold shop. We did so because customers began requesting design assistance for bottles made on "single-stage" manufacturing machines as well as for bottles made on the traditional "two-stage" manufacturing equipment, which was PTI's core expertise. Once we embarked on this pathway, we asked our marketing department to advertise our new capabilities and, I am happy to say, our increased advertising and our new single-stage expertise resulted in several opportunities for PTLLC, as well as for the PTI Process Laboratory.

In 2015 we recognized that we needed additional new equipment to remain relevant in the package development business which led to another partnership with Husky Injection Molding Systems. As a result, Donald Miller and Chris White built an injection molding platform to run a Husky 4-cavity Adapt™ flexible prototyping mold base. The system included a state-of-the-art all-electric Arburg press which was PTI's first all-electric machine purchase. The system was successful but like all new machine technologies, required a long sales cycle to get customers comfortable with the new approach.

I also want to again recognize several key PTI personnel who reached employment milestones during my years as president.

Betsy Brady turned a 'decade older' while I was president, and we held a company picnic in her honor. Here are the words expressed during the ceremony honoring her 30 years of service and her birthday.

"It was a certain irony to me that Florence Henderson, the TV Mrs. Brady, passed away this week and that the TV entertainment shows got reactions from her acting children who obviously have eternal respect for her. If you don't know it, by the way, we at PTI are still known as the "Brady Bunch" by many of our peers in industry, and PTI has its own Mrs. Brady who is the mother figure for us all. Betsy Brady literally has two hundred (PTI) surrogate children that will all have eternal respect for her, just like the TV Mrs. Brady.

Tom gets the credit for launching the business, and there are many of us that get the credit for doing the work of PTI, but Betsy is the one that made it work financially. She worked from the very beginning to manage "The Human Resource (Tom)," and then she also managed all the other PTI human resources, as well as the finances of PTI, often for little compensation during those early years. Betsy is the person that figured out the benefits, the labor laws, the tax filings, and building maintenance, and she was lead negotiator with the Klosters long before we could afford the professional help she provided.

Betsy has also played the role of peacekeeper over the years. I know it is hard to believe, but there were a few times when Tom and one of us did not agree on the way forward, and yes, a few times when Bob or Frank or I would get off track. But we always had Betsy to guide us, and this really was one of the secrets to our success. It is one of my beliefs that people who always agree with one another seldom get anything done, but people who participate and challenge each other often find the breakthroughs and the better way forward. We were fortunate to have our own steady force, Betsy, to keep us focused on always getting better and less focused on getting our own way, and to help us move the business forward. In addition to the sound financial work, the endless pursuit of a better deal on health care and insurance and figuring out how to keep our money at work and out of the hands of the IRS, Betsy contributed immeasurably to our success through her leadership, her steady management style, and her uncompromising ethics.

Betsy also put PTI on the map as a company that supports and uplifts the community. She has served on the boards of Toledo Hospital, ProMedica, the Toledo Community Foundation, and the University of Toledo Foundation, and she has served on the boards and served also as chairman for the Toledo Museum of Art and the Toledo Area Chamber of Commerce. She was President of the Junior League in 1985 and her Carson Family has also been a major supporter of the Boys and Girls Club of Toledo and the Metroparks. Our (PTI's) community involvement not only helps give us purpose, but the connections Betsy and Tom made help us run a better company.

Now that Tom has stepped away from his daily involvement at PTI, we have seen Betsy emerge as an equal co-leader of the company. It is a great asset for us, and for me, to have our chief financial officer with 30 years of experience, help to direct day-to-day activities. Betsy is the leader of employee development and has a hand in the management of PTI's operations as well as overseeing the Family of PTI Companies' business interests. And yes, she is still the chief Peacekeeper."

Scott Steele, 2015

PTI employees have all demonstrated incredible commitment to their jobs over PTI's 35-year history. One particularly memorable story involved a tragic accident that Keith Brown had on his way home one Friday. He left PTI and headed west on Airport Highway and even though he was a very careful motorcycle driver, unfortunately, a car turned across the highway to pull into a gas station and Keith hit him at high speed. Keith was severely injured and taken for emergency treatment. While in the emergency room and probably in great pain, he told the attending physician that he had to let someone at PTI know he wasn't going to be at work on Saturday as he had planned. Keith's family managed to get us the news and as usual, people in the lab willingly stepped in for him and made sure the commitment was covered.

Keith was out for months with his injury and, unfortunately, in his weakened state cancer took its final toll. These are the words expressed by Greg Fisher at Keith's funeral.

"To work with Keith Brown was to be his friend. It was my privilege to know and work with Keith for the past 7 years at PTI, where Keith spent 27 years as the first technician, then as the lead technician, and ultimately as the manager of the analytical testing lab. Keith's impact on PTI runs deep, not just in the lab but throughout the company since many of our senior technical people started their careers at PTI working with him in the lab. Keith was a patient and generous teacher who loved to talk about test methods and equipment….. and about golf …. and about Ohio State football…. and about the latest Star Trek movie…. and about when the Cleveland Browns might finally have another decent season.

Keith was a leader by example who brought out the best in people by inspiring them with the joy that he took in his work and the dedication with which he pursued each task. When I think of working with Keith, I think of him smiling, even during the challenging times.

Keith had a passion for working in the lab, providing answers for our customers, and keeping the equipment running. We all knew Keith as someone who would never give up. He would always make that twenty-seventh check trying to find an evasive small leak in the gas chromatograph. He would usually be the one standing on a step ladder elbows deep in the works of the carbonator trying to get it running again so that he could fill some urgent test bottles for a customer. Keith would never give up.

Keith also had a passion for helping his fellow human beings. He could never seem to believe that he had done enough as the captain of the Friends and Family Battling Cancer ACS Relay for Life team or helping people get through emergencies in their personal lives. No matter how tired or how sick he was, Keith was likely to be the first to arrive and the last to leave when the cause was helping other people. Conversations with him in his hospital room would last for a matter of perhaps a minute or two before he would turn them to "Enough about me, how are you doing? How are things going at work?" Again, no matter how much pain he was in or what he had just been through, Keith would be concerned about others before himself."

Greg Fisher 2016

In 2017 we dedicated the PTI materials testing laboratory to Keith since he exemplified the kind of employee PTI prided itself in.

Marilee and Tim Spann

Sadly, for PTI and during my years as president of PTI, we also lost one of our long-time and most beloved employees; in fact, Tom's very first employee, Marilee Spann. Marilee had been retired for several years but was always willing to come back and fill in as well as come to holiday parties to be with her PTI family. A tree is planted in her honor on the west side of the building.

However, while both the industry and PTI dealt with challenging times and while several of PTI's founders and senior technical employees, including me, opted to retire during or soon after my term as president, I believe we left PTI and the PTI Family of Companies in a sound financial position and ready to meet the demands of a changing world and an evolving packaging industry.

PS: As Founder of PTI, I want to thank Scott Steele, my third "founding" PTI employee, along with Bob Deardurff and Frank Semersky, for accepting the challenge of leading PTI during a period of transition and for inspiring a cadre of newer PTI employees to move PTI successfully into the future – Tom Brady

PTI from 2012 -2022

This story is courtesy of Thierry Fabozzi, PTI President and CEO and formerly Managing Director of PTI-Europe

Thierry Fabozzi

Thierry Fabozzi began his career at Dynaplast S.A., one of the very first European companies to focus on PET packaging.

Founders André-Marcel Collombin and Dr. Glauco E. Curetti created Dynaplast S.A. in Geneva during the 1970's and successfully developed the first injection-compression machine to make preforms as well as developing one of the first successful commercial PET re-heat stretch blow molding machines. Both the Dynaplast injection and blow molding machines where successfully licensed to MAG-Plastic.

Soon after these successful machine developments, and having just graduated from engineering school, Thierry joined Dynaplast as a mechanical engineer to work on two new and important projects, including the development of an aerosol container for Boxal and the development of a new and improved re-heat stretch blow molding machine for Cobarr, one of the M&G companies located in Tortona Italy.

Boxal was a technically advanced aluminum container manufacturer that supplied aerosol containers to a wide variety of industries including for cosmetics, pharmaceuticals, food, and beverages. Boxal was recognized as a world leader in packaging solutions with manufacturing plants principally in France and the Netherlands and was acquired by the Ardagh Group in 2013. Thierry got the opportunity to help develop one of the very first PET container manufacturing machines in the world.

The aerosol project was particularly challenging in that the goal was to use the same aluminum valve on the new PET containers that had been used on regular aluminum containers, and a PET preform provided only a very small neck ring to aid in the handling of the containers during the high-speed manufacturing and filling operations.

Dynaplast began by using a custom-designed single-stage injection-blow molding machine, but eventually

K92 Dynaplast team: Matthew Gehring, Glauco Curetti, André-Marcel Collombin, Thierry Fabozzi.

developed its own DB20/125, a 2-cavity reheat-stretch blow molding machine that could compete at the high manufacturing speeds required for this market segment.

Dynaplast sold most of its machines in Europe for mineral water, and at the time, collaborated with Gerosa, located in Bottanuco, Bergamo, Italy to develop a linear bottle filling machine which could be coupled with the DB20/125 to both form and fill the bottles. Dynaplast sold 15 blow-fill machines during this period and collaborated with Krupp Corpoplast to provide Corpoplast with the same machine, but under a private Corpoplast label.

Dynaplast later added a 3rd cavity to boost output, and eventually Dynaplast developed a 6-cavity ultra-high speed linear machine that could compete with the new linear blow molding machines being produced by competitors.

In 1993, Dynaplast was acquired by Tetra Pak and the headquarters was moved to Geneva Switzerland to become the Plastics Division of Tetra Pak.

Tetra Pak also acquired preform production plants in Belgium (Plastimat) and in Italy (Radici) and the business model that evolved was to supply both preform and stretch-blow molding machines, the same business model that Tetra Brik used to supply the Brik™ machines as an accessory to its carton makers.

Unfortunately, PET converters didn't accept the idea of being locked into an exclusive contract, preferring to have the freedom to shop separately for PET preform and blow molding equipment.

For the record, the Tetra Pak Plastics Division was composed of three divisions, including the PET Packaging Division in Geneva, the Extrusion Blow Molding Packaging Division in the UK, and the Flexible Packaging Division in Lincolnshire, IL, USA, and in India. Tetra Pak's central R&D facility was in Darmstadt Germany and Tetra Pak's blow molding machine divisions were complemented by and supported by Tetra Pak's Barrier and Aseptic groups.

In 1998 Tetra Pak, under Thierry's direction, launched the Tetra Plast™ LX-2, the first commercial reheat-stretch blow molding machine with a servo-stretching system and a proportional pre-blow valve.

It is also noteworthy that the first commercial beer application that employed a plasma SiOx coating (trade named Glaskin™) was also developed by Tetra Pak for Bitburger International, the historic and well-known German brewery.

Tetra Pak, as it happens, also led the development of aseptic filling, including both an in-house linear aseptic filler as well as a rotary aseptic filler developed in cooperation with Rossi & Catelli from Parma Italy.

In 2002-2003 Tetra Pak abandoned its own increasingly less competitive PET preform and stretch-blow molding machinery manufacturing operations to focus on the acquisition of Sidel which had become the world leader in rotary stretch-blow molding equipment.

When Thierry left Tetra Pak in 2000, he moved to Milacron in the US (Ann Arbor, MI) to support the new Milacron reheat-stretch blow molding program, and in 2004 he transferred to the Milacron injection molding group in Germany to focus on caps and closures. During his time in Germany, Thierry led the development of the first injection molding machine dedicated to making beverage caps and closures. The Cap-Tec™ injection molding machine was introduced at the K-Show in 2007.

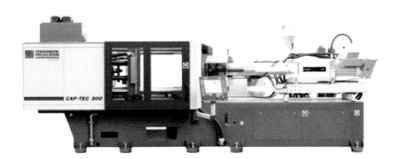

Many years later Husky and Engel followed the movement initiated by Milacron to sell closure-specific injection molding machines with, respectively, the HyCap™ and the E-cap™ machines.

Thierry's Career at PTI

Thierry joined Nestlé in 2008 where he helped lead Nestlé's rigid plastic package development efforts. In 2012 he joined PTI as the General Manager of PTI-Europe where he helped move PTI into the development of the new capsule single service packages that were first commercialized by Nestlé.

In 2017, Thierry moved to the US and took over as CEO for all the PTI Companies, including PTI-USA, PTI-Europe, and Preform Technologies LLC (rebranded as PTI Operations), and he continues in that role in 2022.

Thierry's first year, 2017, turned out to be an unusually interesting year from a both a brand owner's perspective and from a PTI perspective, because the emphasis had shifted from package development to product development, as criticism of fast food and processed food emerged as the new health concern.
At the same time, the worldwide movement against single-serve plastic and the even more famous ocean plastic waste issue emerged, which also had a huge effect on blow molding and aseptic machinery sales, and on PTI's business, which had historically been about developing new packaging for the brand owners.

Almost overnight, NGO's began nightly talk-show appearances and plastic ocean waste emerged as the topic of the day. Some brand owners took the opportunity to show compliance with the new sustainability mantra by claiming to make bottles from ocean waste. At the same time PTI's sister PET recycling division, Phoenix Technologies International, experienced its first ever financial challenges as recycled PET became more expensive than virgin PET, which also was being sold at historically low prices because oil prices had dropped dramatically.

PTI continued to support its customers by light-weighting existing packaging, or perhaps more precisely by "right weighting" existing packaging, since some brand owners had gone too far in downgauging their packaging containers to the point that the packaging would no longer perform its primary function of protecting and dispensing the product.

PTI's material development business also thrived during the period 2017-2020 since plastic material manufacturers brought multiple grades of either bio-sourced resin and/or bio-degradable resin to PTI to be evaluated for processing and for recycling studies.

During this short time frame, many relevant packages were developed by PTI and introduced into the market by the brand owners, including these few name brands that PTI has permission to talk about publicly: FairLife flavored milk bottles, the DrinkWorks cocktail system with pods, and SodaStream's next generation of dishwashing detergent bottles.

The year 2020 began with an even more dramatic and public movement away from single use plastic packaging and during the past two years there have been multiple metro, state, and even federal threats to ban single use packaging ….. and, if that was not enough, COVID also landed! One of our first reactions was to provide our support to the community by making face shields.

Thierry is the first to admit that these unplanned events were a huge challenge for everyone at PTI…trying to navigate the demands for public health and safety while maintaining enough work for the company and still generating enough revenue to pay PTI's employees.

The first Covid lockdown had a huge impact on PTI's container development business, and even though PTI Operations continued receiving orders for household and personal care cleaning product containers, they were unable to fill those orders in a timely way, because of the pandemic.

Interestingly, one of PTI's non-packaging product development opportunities during this critical time was the design and manufacture of plastic face masks to support our local hospitals and health care professionals. Initially, PTI used its 3D printing capabilities to make the masks, but we eventually developed and manufactured a mold to injection mold the masks. We didn't make any money giving away free masks, but we did get huge satisfaction by supporting our community during this difficult time.

At the same time, the pandemic brought to a halt many of the initiatives that had begun to improve both the collection and recycling of plastic. While some programs emerged in the new field of "chemical recycling," the primary issue of collection and getting the consumer involved and committed to participate has still not been addressed. Thus, the high promise sustainability initiatives and goals that had been targeted for 2020 have now moved out to 2030, 2040 and 2050.

Two years ago, PTI sold Phoenix Technologies International to Far Eastern New Century (FENC), the third largest virgin and recycled PET manufacturer in the world, and in 2020 we consolidated our other PTI businesses, with PTI Operations focusing on niche manufacturing and PTI's US and European development operations operating as one business unit.

PTI also strengthened its position in the global PET development market by partnering with SIPA early in 2021and becoming an official member of the SIPA group.

PS: As Founder of PTI I want to thank Thierry for his dedication to making PTI-Europe successful and for his continued leadership at PTI and the PTI Companies as we start a new chapter – Tom Brady

PTI Today

Today, PTI is recognized as a premier PET technical development and support resource in the packaging industry.

Our 36 years of success has only been possible because of great people, starting with the key early team of Bob Deardurff, Scott Steele, Frank Semersky, and Betsy Brady, and continuing with the hundreds of owners, employees, and engineering co-op students who have followed and charted new paths since.

Together, we founded three successful sister companies that are still going strong, including **Phoenix Technologies International, PTI-Europe,** and **Preform Technologies**; we also founded or co-founded a number of joint venture companies with industry partners, including **INOVA Plastics, The Packaging Conference, Guardian Medical USA, Plastic Recovery Systems, Portare Leisure Products, PetWall LLC, Minus Nine Plastics,** and **PTI International**; we created 2 proprietary product businesses, **PTI Instruments** and **PT Healthcare Products**; we developed and/or licensed, sold, or used internally 19 proprietary products, including **Steel Coil Protective Rings, PortaBar™, Tru-Container™, StrataSys™ 3D Printer Material, OxyTraq™, TorqTraQ™, VisiTraQ™, LMS™, MuCell™, oPTI™ Foam Bottles, Virtual Prototyping™, PetWall Profiler™, Smart Blow Molding™, NFA™, PED2000™, SuperGreen™, LNOc™, LNOf™,** and **the Phoenix Process™**.

We are proud to have PTI employee names on more than 150 US and international patents, and we have served virtually every major PET machine and resin supplier, every major US food and beverage brand owner, and we have done business in more than 25 countries around the world.

PTI employees have delivered more than 200 papers and been sponsors at major technical and business conferences, including at the International Society of Beverage Technologists, the Plastics Institute of America, the National Plastics Exposition, and the Society of Plastic Engineers ANTEC Conference, and PTI has been instrumental in the startup and evolution of many of today's technical trade associations, including the Association of Plastic Recyclers, Polymer Ohio, the Toledo Society of Plastic Engineers.

PTI offers a complete array of technical services, including product design, prototyping, and testing, with a complete materials and product analytical testing laboratory, and extensive lab-scale recycling capabilities. PTI also offers manufacturing support services and plastics education and training programs to the industry, and PTI's completely virtual product design and simulation capability has been employed across many industries and for customers who come to PTI specifically to develop and innovate new products.

Through the years, PTI and the PTI Family of Companies have expanded from a one-person office at the corner of Canton and Speilbusch Avenues in downtown Toledo in 1986, to its first rented office and laboratory facility at 333 14th Street in 1987, to our new 10,000 sq ft HQ building at Wolf Creek Executive Park in 1994, followed quickly by our now 52,000 sq ft HQ office/laboratory/storage facility in 1996, also in Wolf Creek, and which is owned by PTI employees. Along the way, facilities were added in Bowling Green and Swanton, OH and Yverdon Switzerland, adding a range of different capabilities.

PTI and PTI employees have also been important contributors to a great many community projects and organizations over our history. PTI remains an important supporter of the University of Toledo and the UT College of Engineering, where many PTI employees and co-op engineering students have trained over the years.

In 2021 PTI, PTI-Europe, and PTI Operations embarked on an exciting future as we became the US and European Technical Partner with SIPA Industries, one of the leading and most innovative packaging equipment and service providers in the world and a long-time PTI ally. SIPA is headquartered in Italy and will now offer PTI sales and service opportunities around the world.

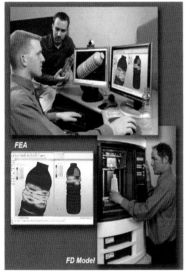 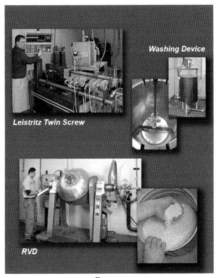 

Design   *Process*   *Test*

DESIGN INNOVATION

We know that speed to market is one of the most important components that drive our client's success in the marketplace. Our specialty is combining top-notch engineering expertise and functional design experts in order to save time and money in the product development and refinement process.

- 3-D Design and Modeling
- Virtual Simulation
- Material Expertise
- Prototype Development
- Limited Production
- Preform Design

SOLVE

Our team of scientists, materials experts and engineering professionals excel at solving our client's toughest challenges; whether in pre-market or existing market products. Through design refinement, plant efficiency studies and virtual simulation, we are able to take on your toughest projects with speed and confidence.

- Material Expertise
- Plant Support and Efficiency Studies
- Recycling Studies
- Injection and Blow Molding Experts

EDUCATE

PTI offers training either on-site or at our global headquarters through our expert instructors who are experienced engineers that are familiar with your team's challenges. Regardless of your plastic packaging area of interest, chances are we already have a class that can benefit you or your employees. If not, we are able to design course-specific studies for our clients when and where it is convenient for them.

- Design of Experiment Tool: Practical Application
- Plastic Packaging for Hot-Fill/Aseptic Beverages
- Technology and Application of PET
- Operator Training: PET Processing

TEST

PTI is where the plastic packaging industry goes for reliable results. Our labs in the US and Europe offer a wide range of testing capabilities on just about any component or aspect of a container. With more than three decades of experience, we are able to provide a confidential and reliable source of testing and analysis to ensure your products are packaged in the best way possible.

- Materials Testing
- Preform and Bottle Testing
- Packaging and Film Permeation Testing
- Closure Evaluations
- Transportation Analysis
- Shelf Life Testing

Let us help you create your next success story.

www.pti-usa.com | +1-419-867-5400

©2018 Plastic Technologies, Inc

DESIGN

SUCCESSFUL PACKAGING DESIGN
...through the combination of aesthetics and engineering.

Producing a commercially-successful product is the objective of every brand owner. Our team of experts understand how important speed-to-market is for our clients. We combine engineering and design expertise to bring functional packages that house your products in the most efficient way possible.

CREATING FUNCTIONAL PACKAGES
...that become commercial success stories.

PTI has taken hundreds of designs from Concept to Commercialization™. Our team of designers, engineers and technicians make sure the knowledge gained from producing prototypes gets communicated to your production floor. We assist you in maintaining the quality and technical specifications for your commercial success.

Sustainable Packaging Innovation.

pti-usa.com

case studies

Value Engineering and Supply Chain Optimization

BACKGROUND: A mid-sized food CPG leverages PTI's packaging supply chain expertise from "transit to shelf" to evade a club chain directive that would have cost $3M in capital equipment upgrades.

ACTIONS: After a thorough technical supply chain review, the CPG returned to the club chain leader and shared the technical data and analysis validating the CPG's packaging solution was the "best-in-class" for the category.

RESULTS: The club chain rewarded the CPG with the incremental business and required the CPG's competition to revise their packaging structures to mimic the design solution of the best-in-class CPG.

Product Life-Cycle Management

BACKGROUND: Mid-sized bakery CPG sought packaging leadership to fill a technical gap within their organization.

ACTIONS: Our packaging engineers were retained to support all marketing, innovation and procurement initiatives. The project scope included new primary and secondary packaging format exploration, plant trials, retail and club store packaging implementations, new vendor feasibility and holiday packaging.

RESULTS: As a result of excellent on-time and quality program implementations, a long-term relationship was established to support the company's ongoing product life-cycle management needs.

Secondary, Tertiary Package Design, Development and Sourcing

BACKGROUND: A consumer product innovator leveraged PTI's engineering skill set to enable the delivery of primary and secondary packaging design and sourcing solutions.

ACTIONS: Our engineers utilized industry best-in-class practices and sourcing relationships to deliver the client's innovation on time, and in full.

RESULTS: The company won a 2014 Global Innovation Award at the International Housewares Show after successfully launching its product within its six-month launch window.

VIRTUAL SIMULATION

SIMULATION MODELING
....reduces time and manages budgets.

PTI provides state-of-the-art technologies and software to help test and refine your concept or product design. We'll make sure your package is ready to meet or exceed performance objectives, with improved speed-to-market and at reduced costs.

By providing virtual prototyping, process simulation, barrier performance modeling and analysis, we complement your entire project team - including design, marketing and production.

PREDICT CONTAINER PERFORMANCE
....before producing a preform.

PTI utilizes virtual modeling software to digitally illustrate the reheat stretch blow molding process. By incorporating elements such as the geometry of the oven, ventilation and machine speed, we can replicate real results with accuracy.

We also utilize Finite Element Analysis to generate an accurate evaluation of the performance of the container by incorporating the thickness distribution and orientation dependent mechanical properties of the container. FEA allows the target performance of the container to be predicted by integrating the geometric design with the virtual profile of wall thickness and orientation-dependent material properties.

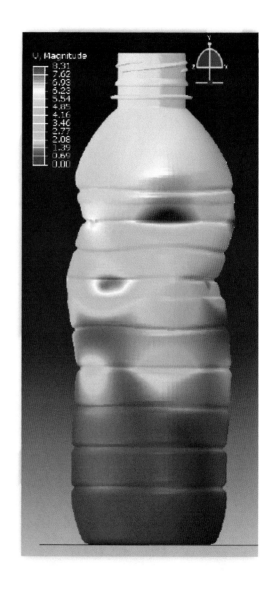

Sustainable Packaging Innovation.

pti-usa.com

120

Take your preform through a virtual trip through a blow molding machine.

By utilizing virtual prototyping tools, your team can prevent the typical production surprises that could be solved through preform analysis and selection. The software is capable of selecting the best preform from all possible configurations by rapidly reheating and blowing each preform design, testing the validity of each style, before fabricating a single preform.

The output of this program is an excellent input for FEA models of the blow molding process. The software is offered as several components; starting with the primary module that generates a complete thermal profile of a preform exiting the oven to a module that designs and optimizes a preform for any inputted container geometry.

Create functional packages that become commercial success stories.

PTI has taken hundreds of designs from concept into production. Our team of designers, engineers and technicians make sure the knowledge gained from producing prototypes gets communicated to your production floor. We assist you in maintaining the quality and technical specifications required for your commercial success.

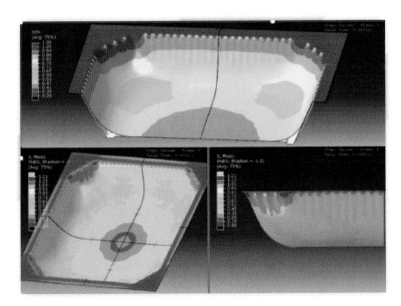

1440 Timberwolf Drive | PO Box 964 | Holland, OH 43528 | 419.867.5400 | pti-usa.com

YOUR DESIGNS IN REAL LIFE
...in as little as 24 hours.

When you need a prototype fast, our team of designers and engineers work quickly to transform your package design to a real life prototype in as little as 1-3 business days. Whether you're looking to define the shape, evaluate squeezability or just visualize your bottle design with filled liquid, a wrapped label, or even a closure attached, we offer a wide range of rapid prototyping options to turn your designs into tangible samples, bringing your designs to life in as little as 24 hours.

Unpolished Translucent Printed Prototype

24 Hour Turnaround: A rigid protoype ready in just one business day. The unpolished printed protoype is great for a visual representation of your package design, but due to rigid nature, cannot be evaluated for squeezability or topload performance. Available in SLA photopolymer.

1-2 Samples: 24 Hours | Cost: $250 - $2,500
20 Samples: 10-20 Business Days | Cost: $15,000 - $25,000

Note: Fill volume may not be accurate and sample will not have filling/capping line placement External dimensions are accurate. Sample is not squeezable and can manually be filled and labelled for visual purposes, but fill volume will not be accurate.

Polished SLA Model Printed Prototype

Five Business Day Turnaround: This clear-view rigid protoype can be ready in as little as five business days. The polished printed protoype is the best 3D printed representation of your transparent package design, but cannot be evaluated for squeezability or topload performance due to its rigid nature. Available in SLA photopolymer and a variety of tints.

1-2 Samples: 24 Hours | Cost: $500 - $3,000
20 Samples: 10-20 Business Days | Cost: $10,000 - $30,000

Note: Fill volume may not be accurate, though external dimensions are accurate. Sample will not have filling/capping line placement. Sample is not squeezable.

Rapid Blow-Molded Prototype

Five Business Day Turnaround: The ideal solution if you have a design ready and you're looking for aesthetic and functional performance from your rapid prototype. This PET prototype is the closest rapid prototype solution to the actual thickness, dimensions, volume of your design and can function similarly to future production samples for topload and squeezability performance.

2-20 Samples: 1 Week | Cost: $10,000
100+ Samples: 1 Week | Cost: $12,000

Note: Available for generic or simple designs. Complex designs or logos may add additional lead time or costs.

1440 Timberwolf Drive | PO Box 964 | Holland, OH 43528 | 419.867.5400 | pti-usa.com

TESTING

Where the packaging industry goes for reliable results.

Our Global Analytical Testing and Production Labs are the heartbeat of our organization; solving performance issues for our customers as well as helping to validate prototype designs and material selection. With more than three decades of experience, we know how to provide the right testing solution for your specific challenge both quickly and confidentially.

Our Analytical and Production Labs specialize in performing independent and confidential testing on the following packaging components:

- Materials
- Preforms
- Bottles
- Closures
- Additional components as needed

Sustainable Packaging Innovation.

pti-usa.com

Color and Spectroscopy

- FTIR Spectroscopy
- UV/Vis Spectroscopy
- FTIR and Raman Microscopy
  - Layer Identification
  - Contaminant Identification

Filled Packages

- In-house filling and processing
- Permeation testing
- Controlled storage and conditioning

Bottles and/or Closures

- Complete in-house characterization and analysis of bottles
- Tandem bottle and closure testing
- Scope of work depends on specific needs, such as:
  - Analysis of test samples versus controll samples
  - Full qualification for machine, process or supplier
  - Long term quality control audits

Analysis of Trace Components

- Materials of interest can be quantified down to parts per million, parts per billion or even lower levels
- Typical components tested include Acetaldehyde, Benzene and Limonene
- GC-MS and GC-MS olfactory are available analysis techniques
- PTI is equipped to develop methods and infrastructure to test for additional compounds as necessary

We can also help offset some of your team's challenges by:
- Becoming an overview resource for your lab's peak demand periods
- Handling routine work which frees your lab for development work
- Taking on the challenging projects - this is what we do best
- Providing an independent, third-party perspective

INTERESTED IN LEARNING MORE?

For a comprehensive list of our standard testing services, or to submit a sample for testing, visit

pti-usa.com/testing

PLANT SUPPORT
& ENERGY OPTIMIZATION SERVICES

Offering a proven approach to improving operational efficiency.

Improving production efficiency and reducing costs is the goal of every business. However, it isn't always easy to identify and ultimately correct the things that are preventing you from achieving those goals. Plus with your staff already busy with their full workload, it can be challenging to find internal resources to accomplish these objectives.

This is where PTI can help. For the past 30 years we have been assisting brand owners and converters to optimize injection and blow molding processes for preform and plastic container manufacturing. We also excel in improving plant operating efficiencies.

Our Process and Energy Optimization approach results in:

- Reduced costs
- Enhanced product quality
- Improved output
- Less waste

PTI
Sustainable Packaging Innovation.

125

COST SAVINGS OPPORTUNITIES

FILLER/BLOW MOLDER SYNCHRONIZATION: Potential energy savings associated with correct machine setup and process can be as much as $170,000 per machine per year.

PROCESSING AND START UP PROCEDURES: By reducing waste at start-up, energy cost-savings between $12,000 and $24,000 dollars a year per machine are possible.

PROCESS REFINEMENT: Depending on the base-line process and oven conditions originally established, another $5,000 to $10,000 a month in energy savings can be achieved. Reducing air usage can result in additional savings that could be up to twice the amount experienced with process modifications.

ACTUAL CLIENT SCENARIOS

SCENARIO 1: Truckloads of parts produced with a premium resin were rejected by the customer jeopardizing future business. PTI was able to solve the problem by improving the process and reducing costs.

SCENARIO 2: A plant installed a new line to produce eight different bottles. Line efficiency was at 41% which caused plant efficiency to be at 68.7%. At the end of the project, plant efficiency was increased to 83.2%. Quality complaints were also reduced.

SCENARIO 3: A brand owner was experiencing bottle expansion. Performance was improved to meet plant standards. Labeling problems were minimized because the bottle expansion was reduced. Package performance improvement enabled a 15% line efficiency increase and reduced lost label scrap by 2% or more.

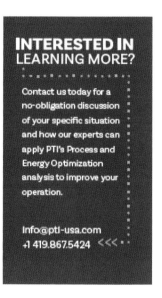

INTERESTED IN LEARNING MORE?

Contact us today for a no-obligation discussion of your specific situation and how our experts can apply PTI's Process and Energy Optimization analysis to improve your operation.

info@pti-usa.com
+1 419.867.5424 <<<

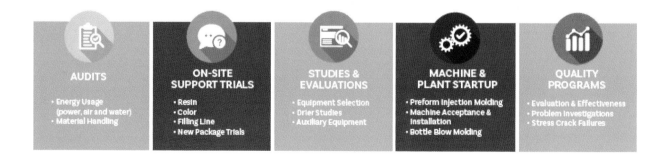

AUDITS
- Energy Usage (power, air and water)
- Material Handling

ON-SITE SUPPORT TRIALS
- Resin
- Color
- Filling Line
- New Package Trials

STUDIES & EVALUATIONS
- Equipment Selection
- Drier Studies
- Auxiliary Equipment

MACHINE & PLANT STARTUP
- Preform Injection Molding
- Machine Acceptance & Installation
- Bottle Blow Molding

QUALITY PROGRAMS
- Evaluation & Effectiveness
- Problem Investigations
- Stress Crack Failures

1440 Timberwolf Drive | PO Box 964 | Holland, OH 43528 | 419.867.5400 | pti-usa.com

EDUCATE

Innovative training...delivered by experts.

Regardless of your plastic packaging area of interest, odds are PTI already has a training module that can benefit you and/or your employees.

Course instructors are industry experts with many years of experience in their respective fields. Most seminars are conducted in small groups in a classroom environment which allows for networking and practical application sessions.

Customized training specific to the needs of your organization is also available and can be modified to accommodate factors such as skill level, niche manufacturing and job role. We are pleased to offer training at your location or in our training hub at our corporate headquarters, whichever is most convenient for you.

PTI
Sustainable Packaging Innovation.

- Technology and Application of PET
- Barrier Technologies and Applications
- PET Recycling
- Aseptic Packaging Technologies
- Thin Wall Barrier Packaging

For more information | training@pti-usa.com | pti-usa.com

TECHNOLOGY AND APPLICATION OF PET

This course provides up-to-date information on PET container technologies and offers the opportunity to discuss your specific applications and questions.

dec 2018
4-6

march 2019
12-14

june 2019
11-13

sept 2019
17-19

oct 2019
15-17

dec 2019
3-5

PLASTIC PACKAGING FOR HOT-FILL / ASEPTIC BEVERAGES

This two day seminar focuses on PET packaging for hot-fill and aseptic filling of low-acid beverages. Covering the basics of non-carbonated packages and examining material compatibility for these types of applications. This course will also cover the most commonly used sterilization techniques as well as new techniques such as high pressure processing. A detailed overview of associated filling technologies will also be provided.

nov 2018
6-7

nov 2019
5-6

HAVE QUESTIONS?
training@pti-usa.com | +1 419.867.5424

READY TO REGISTER?
visit our website: pti-usa.com/hub

Custom classes available by request, at a location convenient to you. Contact us today to learn more!

1440 Timberwolf Drive | PO Box 964 | Holland, OH 43528 | 419.867.5400 | pti-usa.com

PTI Expo Display

PTI Trade Show Display

The Packaging Conference

Phoenix Technologies Trade Show Display

PTI Trade Show Display

Pack Expo Chicago 2019

The PTI Family of Companies

TO VIEW CLICK THE TOPIC BELOW

SERVICES & CAPABILITIES

PLASTIC TECHNOLOGIES, INC.
PHOENIX TECHNOLOGIES INTERNATIONAL LLC
PREFORM TECHNOLOGIES LLC

VIRTUAL PROTOTYPING™ MODULES

PET DRYING & MATERIAL HANDLING

INJECTION MOLD TROUBLESHOOTING

BLOW MOLD TROUBLESHOOTING

PET & PEN RESIN SPECIFICATIONS

PET PHYSICAL CONSTANTS

WE PACKAGE SOLUTIONS®

Phoenix Technologies International (a PTI Company)

Website: https://phoenixtechnologies.net/

PTI "intrapreneurs" who conceived of, created, and ran Phoenix Technologies include Bob Deardurff, PTI VP and Phoenix Technologies CEO, and Don Hayward, PTI Senior Technical Associate and First Plant Manager and General Manager of Phoenix.

Other former O-I/PTI personnel who also assumed major operational roles at Phoenix Technologies include Jack Ritchie, Plant Superintendent, Henry Schworm, Chief Technical Officer, and Dennis Balduff, Principal Engineer.

Sue and Bob Deardurff, Mary Jane and Don Hayward

Operations executives who were important to the success of Phoenix include Ron Ott, Plant Manager and President, Jean Bina Operations Manager, Steve Schultz, Finance Manager, Elaine Canning, Chief Financial Officer, Shari McCague, Corporate Accountant, and Lori Carson, Sales & Marketing Manager, Operations Director, and Site Manager.

Jack Ritchie

Jean Bina & Dennis Balduff

Lori Carson

Elaine Canning

Shari McCague

Henry Schworm

Phoenix Technologies was established in 1992 and is now recognized as a global leader in recycled PET (RPET). The company manufactures clean, consistent, high-grade RPET resin pellets from post-consumer recycled plastic shipped from all over the world.

PET Bottles Containing up to 100% RPET

As the foremost manufacturer of RPET, Phoenix sets the benchmark for quality, technology, service, and overall value. Phoenix's 90,000 square foot, state-of-the-art, Ohio recycling facility was designed from the ground up and produces 80 million pounds of RPET annually.

Using a fine-mesh filtration process or a fine-ground powder process, Phoenix can produce RPET which exceeds the industry's highest standards. Additionally, Phoenix RPET can be used along with virgin bottle resins to create bottles with the right performance attributes for any application. Phoenix Technologies is ISO certified and is continuously introducing new technologies and equipment, enabling it to supply high quality RPET for both food and non-food applications.

Phoenix Flake Washing Plant - Poe Road

By using patented technologies in combination with proprietary blending methods and fine mesh melt filtration systems, Phoenix produces the highest-quality recycled PET (RPET) that customers have come to expect over the past two decades.

Phoenix Pelletizing Plant - Fairview Avenue

Phoenix prides itself on having ultra clean facilities, manufacturing quality products, and having an impeccable safety record. More than a manufacturer, Phoenix thinks of itself as a partner to brand owners and to converters. By leveraging Phoenix's strategic alliances with resin manufacturers, colorant and additive suppliers, processors, bottle producers and sheet extruders, Phoenix can give its customers a competitive advantage.

 In June, 2019, Taiwan-based Far Eastern New Century Corp. (FENC) announced the acquisition of Phoenix Technologies International LLC, Bowling Green, Ohio. Phoenix is a recycler of polyethylene terephthalate (PET) and has the capacity to process 36,000 tons of material each year.

Phoenix is the third production site FENC has acquired in the U.S. over the last several years, including a PET production plant in West Virginia, a research and development center in Ohio and another PET plant in Texas.

Because governments around the world have enacted regulations that require businesses to increase the proportion of recycled raw materials in their products and considering the strong demand for green products in the U.S. market, this acquisition will help FENC's downstream global beverage brand and consumer product clients meet those sustainable development goals. FENC believes that the acquisition of Phoenix will help it to solidify the synergy with its subsidiary in West Virginia as well.

FENC is the world's second largest recycled PET producer and the third largest virgin PET resin supplier. Since 1988, FENC has been conducting R&D on the manufacturing process of recycling and its applications. Its recycling facilities are in Taiwan, Japan, the Philippines, and in the U.S.

Phoenix Technologies From the Beginning

This history is courtesy of Mr. Bob Deardurff, Vice President of PTI and founder of Phoenix Technologies International

Bob Deardurff recalls that the idea of Phoenix Technologies all began during a 1990 meeting he attended in Louisville KY with PTI's customer, Colgate-Palmolive (C-P) and our then primary contact at C-P, Dennis Calabro, to discuss how PTI could support C-P's manufacturing operations.

As Dennis and Bob discussed ways for PTI to help C-P incorporate PureTech Plastic's recycled PET (RPET) flake into C-P's PET bottles, Dennis suggested to Bob that perhaps PTI could best help by pelletizing the then-available PureTech RPET flake so that it would be easier to add into the virgin PET pellets in C-P's bottle manufacturing operations.

An obvious geographical advantage was that PTI was located in Holland OH halfway between Puretech's PET recycling operation in Livonia MI and C-P's bottle manufacturing plant in Cambridge OH.

Of course, PTI had no direct manufacturing experience at the time, but as Bob recalls, the trust that had been developed between C-P and PTI as a development supplier was all that was needed to begin discussions.

Even during that very first meeting, PTI and C-P discussed volume requirements, potential pricing, and they even discussed the idea that an agreement could include an option for C-P to acquire the PTI RPET pelletizing plant in the future.

That first discussion quickly resulted in the decision by PTI to invest in an RPET pelletizing plant but to make that operation a separate PTI business, and to finalize a purchasing contract with C-P which included the option for C-P to acquire the plant in 3 years and at a fair and agreed-upon price, at C-P's discretion.

Fortunately, another former O-I colleague, Don Hayward, was available and interested in leaving his then current employer and coming to PTI to startup and run PTI's first separate company to pelletize RPET, with Colgate as its first contract customer.

In fact, the name "Phoenix Technologies International" was Don's suggestion, and remains the name of the company today!

Because we knew that energy costs would be a factor in site selection, Bob and Don focused on finding a site in the Bowling Green Ohio region. They met first with Sue Clark, the Bowling Green economic development representative who introduced them to Al Green who owned a local property development company, and quickly settled on a site that was owned by Al Green and would allow for future expansion.

To put it in perspective, that first facility was only 10,000 square feet in size and housed only one pelletizing line that could produce 5M pounds of nonfood grade RPET pellets annually. Today, Phoenix Technologies includes 3 facilities at two separate Bowling Green Ohio locations which handle flake washing, pelletizing, decontaminating, packaging, and rail shipping of 80+ million pounds of food grade and nonfood grade RPET annually!

Of course, both Bob and Don had significant experience in starting up plastic manufacturing operations while we were at O-I, but they had never had to figure it all out themselves, and on a "shoestring" budget since we were funding the new operation internally!

So, as Bob recalls, they hopped in Don's trusty used Pontiac Fiero and travelled first to Virginia to investigate the options for purchasing drying and material handling equipment from the Conair Company, then to Pennsylvania to discuss pelletizing equipment with the Gala Company, and finally to Illinois to explore the purchase of extrusion equipment from PTi (we call them PT little i), a global supplier of extrusion equipment.

As they began designing the plant, one of the key design parameters was figuring out how to create and install nonstandard gas-fired flake-drying and pre-crystallizing equipment because energy was going to be the biggest manufacturing cost and gas was then a very low-cost energy resource in Bowling Green Ohio.

And it should also be noted that even though we were starting up our first manufacturing operation and being very stingy about using our own investment funds, Don insisted on purchasing and using new, instead of used, equipment for that first line which turned out to be one of the real keys to our early efficiencies and to the ultimate success and profitability of the operation.

Groundbreaking for the new plant was in December of 1990, followed by installation of equipment beginning in October of 1991 and Bob said that he remembers making our first commercial pellets on December 16, 1991. So, planning and startup all happened within one calendar year, an amazing success, and was all attributable to the energy and commitment of Bob Deardurff, Don Hayward, and to Brian Klausing and Bill Pratt who were hired just as we began the groundbreaking!

Bob and Don also remember hopping into the trusty (used) Phoenix pickup truck and personally delivering the first several gaylords of RPET pellets to the Colgate Cambridge Ohio facility in January of 1992.

When they arrived in Cambridge and opened those first gaylords, Bob recalls that the pellets were still slightly warm from the manufacturing process.

When the Colgate machine operator stuck his arm down into the gaylord and pulled it out to check for fines (powdered PET) on his arms, he immediately said these are really "nice little pellets", and asked "what is the brand?"

Without hesitating and in traditional "Don Style," Don responded "these are our NLP grade pellets (nice little pellets)" which is how the trademarked name NLP™ came about for Phoenix's non-food grade commercial RPET

Shortly after the start up and delivery of those first pellets, Jean Bina, Jack Ritchie, Henry Schworm, and Dennis Balduff all joined Phoenix and helped grow the operation to three extrusion lines and to become a 25M lb/yr operation. Jean handled sales and purchasing, Jack became the plant superintendent, and Henry and Dennis transferred from PTI to handle the engineering end of the business.

By the way, when Phoenix commercialized its **Phoenix Process™** in 1996 to produce food grade RPET pellets, Don also created the brand name for that product, **LNO™** which, as you will appreciate, stands for "Like No Other"!

Today 30 years after startup, Phoenix Technologies is still going strong and is producing more than 80M lb/yr but is owned by Far Eastern New Century, the third largest PET producer and recycler in the world, headquartered in Taiwan with virgin and recycled PET operations in Taiwan, Japan, the Philippines, and in the US.

The Phoenix Technologies Team!

PTI-Europe SARL (a PTI Company)

PTI-Europe was established in 1998 and initially operated as a separate but wholly owned PTI company in Lausanne, Switzerland for the purpose of conducting package and materials development projects for PTI customers located in Europe. In 2003, PTI-Europe moved from Lausanne to picturesque Yverdon-les-Bains, Switzerland and expanded its Analytical Laboratory, adding a joint venture permeability testing laboratory with MOCON Corporation.

Shortly after the move, PTI-Europe added a Recycled PET Laboratory which is available to the industry, and PTI-Europe's PET Technology Training Program is now recognized as a standard industry training program for the European PET industry.

Frank Semersky, Helene Lanctuit, Jean-Claude Baumgartner, Christian Ducreux, Beatrice, Yen Andenmatten, Anne Roulin

Jean-Claude Baumgartner, Sylvie Vaucher, Vincent Le Guen, Yen Andenmatten, Helene Lanctuit, Christian Ducreux

PTI "intrapreneurs" who conceived of, created, and managed PTI – Europe SARL include the late Frank Semersky, PTI VP New Business Development, and Anne Roulin, the first General Manager of PTI-Europe.

Despite the smaller size of the European operation, PTI-E was nevertheless able to bring several innovations to the market and to establish strong relationships with several key global brand owners. One of these early key developments was the first commercial re-heat stretch blow molded PP bottle in Europe, carried out in collaboration with P&G and LyondellBasell Industries, one of the largest plastics, chemicals, and refining companies in the world.

Deep-Grip bottle was another key development, also carried out for P&G, where PTI-Europe not only developed the entire concept at the lab scale but managed the development of the industrial machinery with Sidel.

PTI-Europe also played a major role in the development and qualification of PET recycling technologies, initially by supporting Petcore Europe, the trade association representing the complete PET value chain in Europe since 1993, and by supporting the EPBP (European PET Bottle Platform) organization as a certified testing laboratory. In 2012 PTI-Europe became the first external Mocon Certified Testing Facility

Dana Giorgerini

Christian Ducreux, Greg Fisher, Nicolas Sframeli

When Thierry Fabozzi came from Nestlé to assume the General Manager's role in 2012, he added the thin-wall molding and single serve capsule technologies to PTI-Europe's capabilities. Today Thierry is the President and CEO of the PTI Companies.

Dana Giorgerini, Scott Steele, Stéphane Morier, Thierry Fabozzi, Antonio Farré, Pascal Sandoz, Nicolas Sframeli, Matthieu Larose, Jean-Claude Baumgartner, Christian Ducreux, Florence Baroni, Jean-Luc Roulin, Greg Fisher, Yen Andenmatten, Sylvie Magnin

The Packaging Conference (a PTI joint venture company)

Website: https://thepackagingconference.com

PTI "intrapreneurs" who conceived of, created, and ran the Packaging Conference include the late Frank Semersky, then PTI VP New Business Development and Ron Puvak, then PTI Marketing and Sales Director. PTI's Packaging Conference joint venture partner initially was Container Consulting Associates (CCA) founded by John Maddox, a former technical executive at Eastman Chemical, one of the industry's premier PET resin suppliers.

The Packaging Conference was created in 2008 as a joint venture between PTI and CCA as an annual industry conference that would update industry packaging professionals on the latest innovations in technology, design, and sustainability. Over the years, industry leaders from across the packaging supply chain, including consumer packaging suppliers, resin suppliers, technology providers, equipment manufacturers, and container, closure, and label manufacturers have gathered to facilitate connections and to share the latest consumer packaging innovations.

Networking Opportunities

FUN & CASUAL	FIRST-TIME ATTENDEES	MOST ATTENDED	RISE EARLY	MOST ENGAGED	MOST POPULAR
SUPERBOWL PARTY	WELCOME RECEPTION	NETWORKING RECEPTION	NETWORKING BREAKFAST	NETWORKING LUNCH	NETWORKING REFRESHMENTS
SUNDAY EVENING	MONDAY BRUNCH	MONDAY EVENING	TUESDAY MORNING WEDNESDAY MORNING	TUESDAY AFTERNOON	MONDAY, TUESDAY, WEDNESDAY

The Packaging Conference exhibit area is always the focal point for investigating new technologies, businesses, and ideas. Each of the breakfasts, the morning and afternoon refreshment breaks, the Monday evening reception, and Tuesday luncheon are all designed for maximum networking.

In 2020 CCA became the sole owner of The Packaging Conference, although PTI continues to support what has become the number one annual packaging industry forum.

139

PTI Operations / Preform Technologies, Inc.

Website: http://www.preformtechnologies.com/

PTI "intrapreneurs" who conceived of, created, and managed PTI Operations (initially, Preform Technologies) include Bob Deardurff, Dan Durham, and Jim Sheely.

Preform Technologies, LLC (PTLLC) was formed in late 2003 as a manufacturing company that provides specialty and niche PET preforms and bottles and offers specialty injection molding services for other packaging applications.

In effect, PTI Operations is the extended production arm of Plastic Technologies, Inc. When customers require additional preform or bottle capacity over and above prototyping quantities, PTI Operations supplies those production and pre-production quantities. PTI Operations also specializes in supporting new product market launches and supplies customer special product requirements, including specialty colors or materials.

While PTI Operations, PTI, and Phoenix Technologies can offer design, development, production, and recycle-content preforms and bottles which customers can't get anywhere else from a single source, customers may also order capacities directly from PTI Operations, when those customers have no capacity in house or because the needed quantities are too small to make the customer's own production worthwhile.

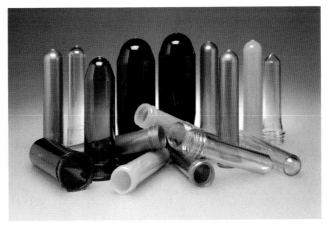

PTI Operations focuses exclusively on supplying specialty packaging, not just commodity items, and the installed injection and blow molding technology for preforms can also be used to manufacture other injection and blow molded parts, in addition to preforms for bottles.

The fleet of PTI Operations machines includes Husky and SIPA injection machines, Sidel SBO and SIPA stretch blow-molding machines, Nissei Single Stage Injection/Blow molding machines, and Bekum extrusion blow molding machines.

As one of the PTI Global family of companies, PTI Operations has an experienced technical team supporting PTI's efforts worldwide. PTI Operations' portfolio includes a long list of PET and polyolefin preform and container success stories.

Having been the silent partner for many key packaging innovations, PTI Operations knows how important confidentiality, performance, and speed are to all customers.

PTI Operations offers a variety of process and product capabilities that can propel customers all the way from "concept to commercialization," and utilizing PTI Operations as a key independent development resource allows customers to take advantage of a variety of tooling and machine capabilities, without having to make a capital investment.

Over its 18 year history, PTI Operations has established itself as the premier manufacturer of technically challenging PET preforms, and also specializes in producing smaller volume PET and polyolefin preforms for food, personal care, and other applications. Additionally, PTI Operations can provide smaller quantity runs of injection, extrusion, or reheat stretch-blow-molded containers.

PTI Operations' extensive capabilities also can be used for emergencies or for smaller preform runs when customers don't want to disrupt their own production, including assisting with:

- Production quantities - technically challenging preform production.
- Resin trials - multiple materials and small run volumes.
- Test market quantities - 500,000 to 5 million preforms.
- Overflow volumes - 10 to 20 million preforms per year via predictable monthly draws.
- Emergency runs - unforeseen and emergency supply issues.
- Container production - small quantity runs of injection, extrusion, or reheat stretch blow-molded containers using PET, PP, HDPE and other resins.

Guardian Medical USA

Toledo Mayor Michael Bell, Tom Brady, Betsy Brady, UT President Dr. Lloyd Jacobs, UT Engineering Dean Dr. Nagi Naganathan

UT Professor of Bioengineering, Dr. VJ Goel, Renowned Spinal Surgeon and Founder of Spinal Balance Dr. Anand Agarwal, Tom & Betsy Brady, PTI Chief Technical Officer Tracy Momany, ProMedica CEO Randy Oostra

In 2017 after I was finished judging the University of Toledo College of Engineering Freshman Design Competition presentations which took place in the Brady Engineering Innovation Center at the University of Toledo, I was approached by Dr. Anand Agarwal who I had never met before and who asked if I was interested in learning about a new plastic packaging development that Dr. Agarwal and his team at Spinal Balance, a startup medical device company, were pursuing. Spinal Balance was in UT's Entrepreneurship Incubator in the same building as the Engineering Innovation Center, so my answer was an instant "for sure," and off we went to see what Spinal Balance was all about.

As an experienced and world-renowned spinal surgeon, Dr. Agarwal realized that regulators, insurance providers, and hospitals were driving a transition from the standard industry practice of using orthopedic implants that must be sterilized before each procedure, to implant systems that were sterile packaged, to decrease risk, reduce costs, and meet changing regulatory requirements. As these requirements were just beginning to take effect, the entire industry was being forced to replace the then-current non-sterile and unlabeled implants with packaged sterile implants.

Dr. Agarwal explained that sterile tube packaging virtually eliminates the risk of seal failures, saves inventory space, is intuitive to use, and saves surgical time as well as providing the required traceability of individual parts from the time of manufacture to patient delivery by using a Unique Device Identification (UDI).

As we considered the opportunity, we learned that the global market for medical implant sterile packaging was already valued at $1.5 billion and was expected to grow to $2.7 billion by 2025, and that even though there were already several sterile package suppliers for orthopedic implants, sterile "tube packaging" for orthopedic implants was the trend, and that Dr. Agarwal and Spinal Balance had just developed and applied for patents on a unique and (he believed) superior sterile medical tube packaging design.

However, Dr. Agarwal also realized that Spinal Balance did not have the plastics expertise to develop and manufacture his proprietary sterile packaging, but after hearing me talk about plastic manufacture during the judging competition, he correctly concluded that perhaps PTI and Spinal Balance could form a joint venture company to produce Spinal Balance's patented sterile packaging, which is exactly what we did!

Off course, PTI had no expertise or contacts in the medical industry, even though we knew there was huge opportunity in medical packaging, and Spinal Balance had no expertise in plastic package design and manufacture, even though that is what Dr. Agarwal needed to commercialize his ideas!

Within a matter of several months, we got to know each other, and we agreed to form a joint venture company to design and manufacture the proprietary packaging for Spinal Balance and for the industry generally.

We named our new company Guardian Medical USA and located the new company in space leased from PTI's Preform Technologies LLC manufacturing company which had both injection and blow molding capacity, and we contracted with PTI to do all the design and prototyping of our developing product lines.

Guardian designed and installed a clean room and quickly got up to speed on the rigors of FDA approvals which, of course, was where Spinal Balance's medical product experience was essential.

Tracy Momany, a 30-year seasoned expert in plastic package development and the former Chief Technical Officer at PTI is now the CEO and Betsy Brady who operated most recently as Interim CEO is now Board Chair. Don Kennedy, with 40 years of experience in the medical industry, is VP of Sales and is contacting medical device companies seeking sales opportunities. Natalie Holobaugh, with prior operating experience at Amazon, is the Operations Manager and has been instrumental in the creation of Guardian's quality control and production systems.

Sales and numbers of customers are projected to grow rapidly and the goal of finding a strategic buyer within the medical industry looks extremely promising. As of this writing, the Guardian leadership team has secured additional venture capital investment funding which will move this startup to the next level.

Advantages of Tube Packaging

Less waste, easier package access, more space efficiency, improved user safety, and better labeling

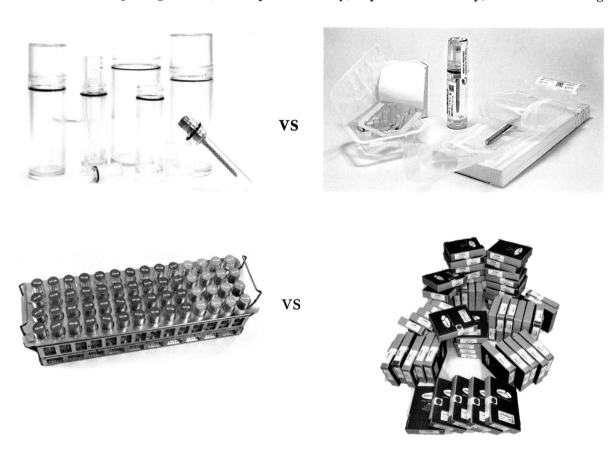

Industry Publications Documenting PTI's Businesses

Entrepreneurial Spirit Molds Plastic Technologies' Success

From Industry Week, Sept 2, 2015

By Michele Nash-Hoff

https://www.industryweek.com/leadership/companies-executives/article/22008099/entrepreneurial-spirit-molds-plastic-technologies-success

Founder Tom Brady says any employee at PTI can be considered by the management team for an opportunity to buy an equity stake. Some 40% of PTI employees are owners today.

During a recent tour of manufacturing plants in the Toledo, Ohio region, I decided to write an article about Plastic Technologies, Inc because of the interesting story about Dr. Tom Brady who founded the company in 1985. Brady worked for Owens-Illinois, Inc. from 1971-1984, and became the vice president and director of plastics technology.

He led the development of the first PET (polyester) plastic soft drink container and directed the technical activities for all of O-I's plastic product lines.

147

Asked what led him to start PTI, he said, "In late 1985, I happened upon a unique opportunity to start the company. Several of the major Coca-Cola bottlers were seeking to expand their already successful PET bottle manufacturing operations and to develop new and innovative PET plastic soft drink packaging products. The four largest Coca-Cola regional bottling cooperatives agreed to jointly sponsor and fund product development and engineering projects, and they approached me to manage those project development efforts. Not having an interest in just changing jobs, I made a counteroffer to those Coca-Cola cooperatives to establish a separate independent company for the purpose of managing their projects. When they agreed, I left O-I to start Plastic Technologies, Inc. and signed long-term contracts with all four Coca-Cola cooperatives.

"Because of my industry experience, I was quickly able to identify additional customers that were non-competitive to Coca-Cola and I hired a small, but highly experienced professional staff, to do the technical development for the Coca-Cola cooperatives and for other customers," Brady continued.

"Because of our professionalism and experience, we were quickly able to establish a reputation in the industry as a high-quality PET R&D and technical support company.

As our technical staff expanded and our revenue grew at compound annual rates of 35%, we moved to a larger facility in 1989 and set up both analytical testing and process development laboratories, with the capability of prototyping and testing PET containers and preforms. We founded Phoenix Technologies International LLC in 1991 in nearby Bowling Green, Ohio and have since then expanded the plant three times to produce recycled PET using proprietary technology.

"Because PET had become the material of choice for new packaging during the 80s and 90s, we were able to quickly expand our customer base and to become involved in developing many different products and businesses, including health care packaging, plastic recycling, specialty compound development and even leisure products. Our experiences outside the PET packaging field provided a basis for us to hire additional technical professionals to staff our laboratories and establish a reputation in the plastics industry as a substantial technical development company.

"Since those early days, we have developed relationships with most major manufacturers, resin suppliers, machinery builders, brand owners, and converters. Today, we even supply preforms for blow molding to customers needing specific quantities or unusual designs. We have also learned how to work effectively with competitive customers, and we have become recognized for our excellence in protecting customer intellectual property and confidentiality. Today, our customers are involved in every step of the PET value chain from raw material supply through end-of-life recyclability."

I asked if they were affected by the recession of 2008-2009 and if so, what did they do to survive it? Brady said, "The recession did have a big effect on PTI's business, but the recession, per se, was not the most significant issue. Rather, the recession just added to the challenge of changes that were already happening in the world at large."

As is true for almost every business today, one of the challenges for PTI today is to redefine its business going forward. Brady said that what PTI has done successfully for 30 years is no longer as different and special as it once was. The challenge for PTI, and for every business today, is to find the "gaps" in the markets of the future that can be filled by employing the experience and knowledge that has been developed over many years.

Brady did say that "we had to do some things differently during the recession. We had to get more professional about sales because there are many more companies selling the same technologies and services now. The biggest impediment to our continued growth is that there are more competitors, so that staying ahead of the competition is a bigger challenge." When he started the company, he was working with the top levels of management at his major customers. Now, he says that business is being done at a different level. More business is handled today by professional purchasing agents, so you have to be more price competitive than in the past. They also went through formal training in Lean, which has been beneficial to their manufacturing businesses, because, he says, "You have to be more efficient to be competitive in every aspect of your business today." However, the Lean initiative didn't affect PTI's testing lab, where becoming ISO certified had more of an impact.

Since I had seen a whole wall of patents PTI had been granted on display at their headquarters, I asked if the change in patent law under the America Invents Act of 2011 affected his company. He replied, "We have to take the steps to be 'first to file' instead of being able to rely on being 'first to invent.' We have to file more provisional patents than we ever had to in the past, which adds another big burden and costs that we didn't have previously. Our number of patent applications has shrunk now that we can't depend on being first to invent. Anything that adds bureaucratic activity becomes a burden on business."

After my visit, I had emailed Brady information on the proposed patent legislation (H.R. 9 and S.1137) and asked if these bills would have an effect on his company. He responded, "You don't have time to fight everything that comes up. You try to work around it. In fact, we find that patents are less valuable than they used to be. It is more important to be first to the market and to be innovative. Our growth hasn't been about becoming a bigger and bigger company. We started Phoenix Technologies and our other companies so that those teams could be more entrepreneurial themselves. Our growth model has been to expand by creating our own 'Intrapreneurs,' by offering those intrapreneurs ownership and by growing as a family of companies.

Our PTI family of companies now includes two manufacturing companies, two technical development and engineering service companies and three joint venture companies that license technology or sell specialty services to the packaging industry (Preform Technologies LLC, Phoenix Technologies International LLC, PTI Europe SARL, PETWall LLC, Minus 9 Plastics LLC and The Packaging Conference). Today, many PTI employees are owners and are in a position where they can truly feel it's their company. Any employee can be considered by the management team for an opportunity to buy an equity stake, and 40% of PTI employees are owners today. We have more than 200 employees worldwide and many of the products you buy every day are sold in plastic containers designed by one of our companies."

During my visit, I was astonished to learn that there are only 10 states that have bottle deposit programs to encourage recycling — California, Connecticut, Delaware, Hawaii, Iowa, Maine, Massachusetts, Michigan, New York, Oregon, and Vermont. In these states, about 80% of bottles are recycled, while in non-bottle-deposit states only about 20% of bottles are recycled.

Asked why more states don't have bottle deposit programs, Brady responded that many major companies oppose the programs because they say it would add to their costs.

He explained, "You have to have an infrastructure in place to get enough material to make recycling profitable." However, he emphasized that everybody, even those who think deposit systems cost more money, would win if there was more recycled material, because the costs for virgin material would go down. He also pointed out that a lot of the recycled material goes offshore to China and other Asian countries because it is cheaper to ship the material in the empty containers that are going back to Asia than it is to ship the material to Ohio.

"We are a big enough company that we can buy recycled material from other sources in Mexico, Canada, South America, and even Iceland; and we also benefit because we put it back into the highest value end-use products — food and beverage containers," said Brady, who pointed out that when China and India get to our standard of living, there isn't going to be enough of all the raw materials to go around.

That means that reusing all materials will eventually become necessary and that recycling will become a significant industry, rather than remaining a "nice thing to do."

In 2009, Brady took a leave of absence from the company to become the interim dean of education at the University of Toledo. He said, "At first, I was judged by the faculty and staff at the college to be a poor choice as the interim dean. However, I actually had the advantage of being completely dependent upon the expertise and experience of the faculty and staff at the college. I made a personal commitment to get to know each and every person in the college and to understand the personal and professional backgrounds of everyone. As a result, we were able to work together to craft a mission and strategy for the future and to create a climate of success going forward."

Therefore, I wasn't surprised to learn that Brady's grandfather founded the University of Toledo's college of secondary education. His mother, an aunt, his two sisters and both grandmothers all taught school. He doesn't just "talk the talk," he "walks the talk." When he was interviewed by Plastic News prior to being inducted into the Society of Plastics Industry Hall of Fame in, 2012, he said, "My goal is to help anywhere I can to make education better. If we don't educate our kids in this country, we're lost.

Our only competitive advantage is being able to be entrepreneurs. The rest of the world can catch up in everything else, so we better figure it out. And there are not going to be enough unskilled jobs in the future, so you better educate people so they can go out and create their own jobs."

Dr. Brady emphasized the importance of education and training to economic development. "In a sense, I think I could reduce the entire economic development issue to just this one issue. That is, if we spent every one of our economic development dollars on building a world class PreK-20 education and training system, I truly believe that economic development would happen naturally as a by-product of that initiative." He reiterated a point that he had made to the mayor of Toledo a few years earlier:

- Higher per-capita income is a by-product of higher-paying jobs
- Higher-paying jobs are a by-product of knowledge-based commerce
- Knowledge-based commerce is a by-product of education and talent
- Talent and education are by-products of a superior K-16 school system, substantive trade and skill development institutions, and a superior teaching and research university.

I completely concur and made similar points in my book, "Can American Manufacturing be Saved?" Why we should and how we can, as well as the several blog articles I have written about workforce development and attracting the next generation of manufacturing workers.

Manufacturing jobs are the foundation of our economy and the middle class. We must strengthen our manufacturing industry to create more jobs if we want our children and grandchildren to have an opportunity to live the "American Dream."

PTI in the News

Toledo-based PTI Leads Plastic Packaging, Recycling Industries

Published in 2009 by The Toledo Free Press
Written by Duane Ramsey, Senior Business Writer
news@toledofreepress.com

A Toledo group of companies known as PTI develops plastic packaging and plastic package recycling for major companies like Coca-Cola and Colgate-Palmolive. Plastic Technologies Inc. (PTI) and its family of related companies are a privately-owned business that develops plastic containers for Coke and for Colgate and for many other consumer product companies at its Toledo headquarters, where it conducts research and develops manufacturing processes.

Another PTI company, Phoenix Technologies International, is the world's largest producer of recycled plastic resins used in the production of clean plastic bottles and containers for Coke, Colgate and for other customers, PTI officials said.

It all began in the 1980s when a young plastics engineer named Tom Brady was asked to develop plastic bottles for Coke. While serving as Vice President of Plastics Technology at Owens-Illinois Inc., Brady led the development of the first plastic soft containers made of polyethylene terephthalate, known as PET, now the most recycled plastic packaging material in the world.

When O-I decided not to invest in the plastic container business at that time, Brady took the proverbial leap of faith, left O-I and started PTI in 1985.

Today, PTI employs more than 200 people worldwide and is the leading PET packaging development resource in the industry.

"When it comes to PET containers, PTI is the premier development company and has clients around the world. That speaks very highly of their expertise in that industry," said Dr. Saleh Jabarin, director of the University of Toledo College of Engineering Polymer Institute.

Jabarin and Brady were colleagues in plastics technology at O-I and were also undergraduate classmate students of engineering at Dartmouth College. After Brady left O-I, he helped Jabarin establish the UT Polymer Institute which involved moving the entire O-I Plastic Development Laboratory to UT.

It's not the only connection PTI has with the UT. Brady said that 4 of the company's 7 vice presidents and a third of all its employees are graduates of business, engineering or science programs at UT.

Brady also serves on the UT Board of Trustees and chairs the external affairs committee, which oversees technology transfer and commercialization. He also sits on the Ohio governor's Third Frontier Advisory Board and on the board of directors of the Regional Growth Partnership, SSOE Inc., the Toledo School for the Arts and Toledo Symphony.

Brady says that "The secret to corporate success is hiring people who are smarter than you and then getting out of their way." He also says and believes that "Entrepreneurial activity is not about having everything laid out in front of you. Rather, it's about taking the playing field you have and then making something out of it."

Brady says that "You have to have a strategic plan but, you must also go where the business takes you. You must diversify while specializing and while also adding intellectual capacity. Our success has also been about building a business that provides full-service and unparalleled knowledge and we have focused on offering the shortest response time in the plastic packaging industry."

Brady's company developed the first plastic bottle for Coke and has designed all subsequent plastic containers for Coke, Brady said. The combined PTI companies provide research, development, design and prototyping capabilities for Coke, Colgate and for many other household and industrial product users.

One of PTI's companies, Perform Technologies, manufactures small-to-medium production runs of plastic bottles and containers at its Toledo facility. Preform Technologies also produces specialty injection-molded packaging products and pre-forms for bottle manufacturing.

As another service to the industry, PTI also develops equipment, instruments, and provides manufacturing support and training to the plastic packaging industry.

PTI-Europe, located in Yverdon les Bains, Switzerland, provides the same plastic development services and products to Coke and to other PTI clients in Europe. And PTI also operates two investment and technology licensing companies to support its other businesses.

Most recently, PTI formed The Packaging Conference LLC, a joint venture company which will sponsor annual international conferences for the packaging industry. Brady said the first conference was hosted Feb. 4 in Las Vegas, which attracted 180 persons from 100 companies.

Brady said PTI is in the process of a management/ownership transition that will result in him and his wife, Betsy, vice president of finance, administration and chief financial officer, maintaining 40 percent ownership with its officers and employees owning the remaining 60 percent of the company

PTI's newest executive, Craig Barrow, recently joined the management team as Vice President and Chief Operating Officer, and will transition to President of PTI, when Brady becomes Interim Dean of Education at UT later this year.

"There is no shortage of innovation at PTI. Remarkable things are happening without any lack of imagination," he said.

Another PTI company, Phoenix Technologies, located in Bowling Green, Ohio, utilizes proprietary technology developed by PTI to prepare post-consumer recycled PET for applications in food and non-food packaging.

Phoenix was the first U.S. PET recycling company to receive FDA approval for manufacturing recycled food-grade plastic from recycled PET in 2001.

PTI also recently unveiled the first commercially produced plastic bottle made of 100 percent recycled PET resin, which is safe for direct food contact.

The 100,000-square-foot plant in Bowling Green produces 80 million pounds per year with 75 employees working in shifts round the clock, said President and CEO Bob Deardurff. The recycling process recovers about 3 plastic bottles for every person in the United States. "The biggest challenge is getting the raw materials," said Deardurff, who was the first professional to join Brady at PTI in 1986 and is a graduate of the UT College of Engineering.

Phoenix Technologies buys clean bottle flakes made from recycled plastic bottles. It then cleans, processes, and produces PET pellets that are shipped in bulk to plastic bottle and container makers across the country.

Phoenix installed additional production capacity last fall for the next generation of recycled PET that PTI is currently developing, Deardurff said.

PET Bottle Pioneer Brady Lends Imagination to Education

Bill Bregar
Plastics News, April 2, 2012

Dr. Tom Brady, chairman of PET packaging research and development firm Plastic Technologies Inc., is full of creative ideas about plastic bottles — and the future of American education.

In 2009, Brady took a bold step for an industrialist. He accepted the invitation of University of Toledo President Lloyd Jacobs to become interim dean of UT's college of education.

That level of community activism comes naturally for Brady. He also is active in Toledo schools, both public and charter, and serves on the boards of the Regional Growth Partnership Board and Ohio's Third Frontier program.

Oh, by the way ... his company helped create the contour PET Coke bottle, and other landmark packages.

Now Brady reaches another landmark, as he joins the Plastics Hall of Fame. The native of Maumee, Ohio, explained his wide-ranging interests in an interview at PTI in Holland, near Toledo.

PTI is exhibiting this week at NPE2012, at Booth 7253.

Brady got in on the ground floor of PET soda bottles, joining Owens-Illinois Inc. in 1972 as senior scientist in plastic materials and processes. The three other PTI co-founders also worked at O-I: Scott Steele, named president earlier this year when Brady became chairman; Bob Deardurff, president of sister company Phoenix Technologies International LLC, a PET recycler; and Frank Semersky, who recently retired as vice president.

Steele nominated Brady for the Plastics Hall of Fame.

"I, along with Bob and Scott and a number of other people at Owens-Illinois, were literally responsible for starting up our manufacturing operations in the beverage business, between 1976 and 1984," Brady said. "Remember, O-I had never made PET bottles. It was a whole new business."

Brady earned a master's degree in materials science from Dartmouth College. After getting a doctorate from the University of Michigan in engineering plastics materials, he joined Owens-Illinois.

O-I was a whirlwind of activity. He helped set up its first PET blow molding plant, in Milford, Conn., followed by factories in Maryland, Alabama, California and Canada, all in a five-year period.

A major glass-container manufacturer, O-I was already into plastics, but it was all polyethylene, PVC and polystyrene bottles for household products. PET soda bottles were new and exotic.

155

"When I walked in, very quickly it was: How do you get stuff in machines and make bottles out of it? And that was the interesting thing.

We went from being literally new engineers to experienced people in a matter of a few years, because there was nobody else. We went and did it. We invented the machines. We designed the bottles. We invented the processes."

Brady rose to become vice president and director of R&D.

Meanwhile, led by John Dunagan, a Coke bottler in Texas, bottlers were setting up in-house blow molding. Eventually, several bottlers would become giants of self-manufacturing such as Western Container Corp., Southeastern Container Inc., Apple Container Corp. and FlorPak.

Dunagan offered Brady a job in 1984. Intrigued, he knew it was a pivotal moment.

"There were probably literally 10 people in the world that knew as much as I did about PET. How many times in your life do you end up being in the right place at the right time? But I really didn't want to go work for somebody else again," he said.

Instead, Brady decided to leave Owens-Illinois and start his own firm. The first client: Coca-Cola Co. and the bottlers. PTI was born in 1985.

Early projects were multilayer PET containers with an ethylene vinyl alcohol barrier layer and a plastic soda can. Light weighting was a major push.

"We saved Coke millions and millions of dollars, just taking weight out of the preform," Brady said.

PTI began a long-term relationship with Colgate-Palmolive Co., designing its new PET containers for consumer staples like liquid hand soaps, laundry detergent and dishwashing liquid.

Today PTI has more than 200 customers. The company employs about 200 people, 100 of them in the Toledo area.

"This is really the premier provider of package technology and materials-development services for the industry. And we work for everybody," he said. PTI's walls are adorned with plaques detailing 140 patents.

Brady said PTI has kept its entrepreneurial roots. About 50 of the 200 employees have ownership stakes in PTI or its six sister companies, which include Phoenix Technologies, Preform Technologies LLC, PETWall LLC, Minus 9 Plastics LLC and The Packaging Conference.

The firm is active in bio-resins and nanotechnology.

Education: Walking the walk

Lots of business executives complain about America's education system. Brady gets directly involved.

"My goal is to help anywhere I can to make education better," he said. "If we don't educate our kids in this country, we're lost. Our only competitive advantage is being able to be entrepreneurs. The rest of the world can catch up in everything else, so we better figure it out. And if you hope you get a job at Chrysler, that's one thing. But if you educate people, they'll go out and create their own jobs."

His grandfather founded the University of Toledo's college of secondary education. His mother, an aunt, his two sisters and his grandmother all taught school.

Toledo is one of the leaders in Ohio in vocational education.

Brady was a founding board member of the Toledo Technology Academy. PTI welcomes interns from the school.

Brady said he feels strongly that not everybody needs to go to college. But young people do need some post-secondary training. "There are lots of jobs out there — welding, machine technology, process controls, electrical technicians, computer technicians, you name it — that don't require four years of college."

He serves on the boards of Toledo Early College High School and the Toledo School for the Arts.

His wife, Betsy, is a trustee and past chairman of the Toledo Museum of Art.

Tom Brady is active in a major effort in Toledo schools to create a STEM program (science, technology, engineering and mathematics) all the way from kindergarten through high school.

Brady calls his two years as interim dean of UT's college of education "one of the most satisfying things I've ever done." At first, he had some doubts. So did the faculty.

"I was an engineer, not a guy from education. And they said, 'Here's a guy who's all about profit; we're about mission.' I mean, I had three strikes against me."

Brady left PTI to become dean in 2009 and 2010. He spent time getting to know the professors personally. He worked hard to meet all the area school superintendents. He made connections with local business leaders. Brady thinks education can benefit from fresh thinking. Too often, the education establishment gets "inbred," he said. "It gets to be very defensive about itself," he said.

"One of the things that happens in the private sector is, there's lots of crossover. People go back and forth. You know what's going on in your industry and other industries. And what I became convinced of is, we need more people to get into education that haven't been in it."

Tom Brady's Home Plastic Packaging Museum

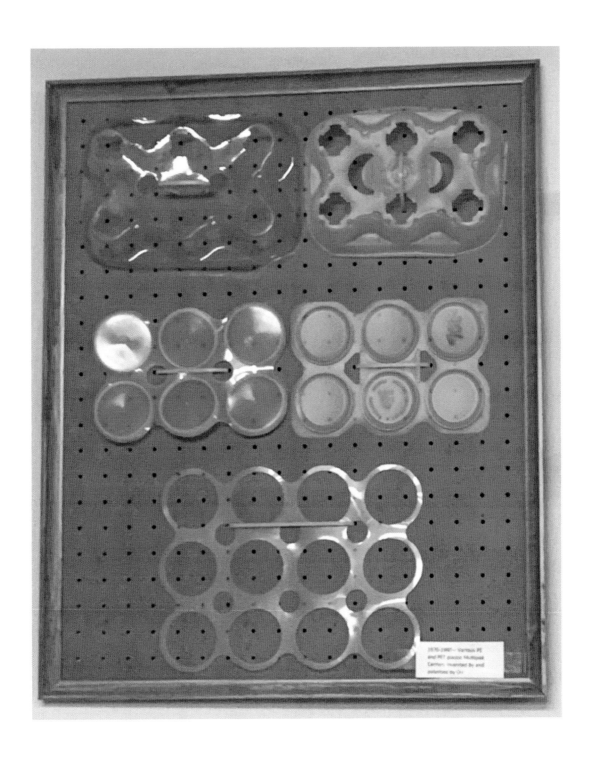

The Future - The Case for a Circular Economy

Courtesy, in part, of The Sustainability Institute
(https://www.sustainability.com/thinking/creating-a-circular-economy-for-plastics/)

A circular economy is restorative and regenerative by design. This means materials constantly flow around a 'closed loop' system, rather than being used once and then discarded. In the case of plastic, this means simultaneously keeping the value of plastics in the economy, without leakage into the natural environment. The Ellen MacArthur Foundation reported that more than 40 years after the launch of the first universal recycling symbol, just 14% of the plastic packaging used globally is recycled, while 40% ends up in landfill and 32% in ecosystems, with the remaining 14% used for incineration or energy recovery. To move society away from the "take, make, dispose" mindset that has long-informed business models, a fundamental rethinking is required which will involve a) improving recycling, b) promoting reuse, and c) creating a market for recycled materials and redesigning products with end of life in mind.

While it is true that "the future belongs to those who prepare for it today," I believe that the opportunity for the plastics industry is to support and create products and systems which will "incentivize the consumer and industry to participate."

Technologies and systems for reuse of all materials, including plastics, are important and crucial but, with 7.5B people already on this planet and with world population projected to increase to 11B people by 2050, and with our current waste disposal and resource issues having resulted from "disincentivizing" the people on this planet to engage in a "circular economy," I believe that, in addition to innovative product and waste disposal technology developments, we must also develop and implement incentives to motivate or force people to engage in making a circular economy happen.

Without offering a comprehensive review of the global plastics waste disposal issue, I will summarize my proposed guidelines for creating a viable future circular plastics economy.

1) Start with national deposit legislation which will increase the plastic PET bottle recycling rate from 30% to 70% and the number of pounds recycled from 3B to 5B, almost overnight! Today, 80+% of containers are returned in the (only) 10 deposit states while (only) 15-20% are returned in the 40 non-deposit states.

2) Follow that with a voluntary bottle/bag/ other return system that is sponsored by the plastics industry, and which would handle all packaging plastics. Check out the comprehensive voluntary return system that is already happening in Ann Arbor, MI at: https://www.recycleannarbor.org/services-guide/plastic-pollution-solution)

3) Follow that with state-sponsored programs to build (some) roads and (some) building materials out of mixed recycled plastics, as they have done in Australia and the Netherlands. Road and walkway paving (as a replacement for asphalt) and building blocks (as a replacement for cement) appear to be feasible solutions to using the mixed plastics waste stream, after we remove and recycle the high value PET and PE. In fact, there is a case for adding in crushed glass and other waste materials, using the mixed thermoplastics as a matrix and, using not-easily-recyclable plastics would solve the film and multilayer plastics issue. Early results suggest that mixed and not-easily-recyclable plastics could be used as high volume, durable, economical, and functionally appropriate, bulk paving and building materials and, if you search the Internet, you will find pilot projects that are well-along in Australia and the Netherlands. See, for example:

https://www.betterworldsolutions.eu/portfolio/road-recycled-plastic/   https://www.byfusion.com/byblock/

4) Create a returnable plastics lottery system where reverse vending machines are used as slot machines and where any (authorized) plastic item could be deposited and where only very occasionally would the depositor win a (relatively) large dollar amount prize. The lottery mentality has been proven over many years to work effectively. That is, virtually everyone will consider buying a lottery ticket, knowing that the chance to win is 300 million to 1 but, also knowing that there is only a (small) chance to win big. I guarantee you that a lottery system will bring back whatever plastic items we want to collect, just as deposit systems guarantee a high return rate for bottles. With a lottery system, we could include all types of plastic items; bottles, straws, cups, lids, plastic bags, whatever! Reverse vending machines that can identify and grind various plastics are already commercially available and every state has a lottery commission. Why not try it?

5) Finally, do everything possible to promote new technologies for recycling and to make recycling a profitable business opportunity.